Sushi Secrets was written by Chihiro and Kazuko Masui

Photographs by Stephen J. Black and Richard Haughton

Editorial directors / Frédérique Sarfati and Dominique Dumand

Production / Isabelle de Jaham

Graphic design /

Page layout / Émilie Greenberg

Copy reading / Élizabeth Guillon and Odile Zimmermman

© Hachette Livre 2004
This edition published by Hachette Illustrated UK, Octopus Publishing Group Ltd,
2–4 Heron Quays, London E14 4JP

Editorial of English edition by JMS Books LLP (email: moseleystrachan@blueyonder.co.uk)

A CIP catalog for this book is available from the Library of Congress

ISBN-13: 978-1-84430-128-7

ISBN-10: 1-84430-128-1

Printed in Singapore by Tien Wah Press

SUSHI SECRETS

PREFACE

I have known Kazuko Masui for almost thirty years. When we first met, her daughter Chihiro was about ten years old. At the time, my career as a fashion designer had just taken off. My show in New York and my shop in Paris were unexpectedly successful. Kazuko came to see me with the editor of a well-known Japanese fashion maga-zine. We hit it off immediately and found a common interest: good cuisine!

When Kazuko told me she was writing a book on sushi with her daughter, I thought it was a wonderful idea. It was a new concept: nobody had thought of associating the viewpoints of two generations of sushi lovers. Kazuko is a purist. For her, sushi is classical art. She has never made sushi herself—"impossible," she says. I think she has never even tasted a California roll. Chihiro has obviously tasted all the best sushi in the world with her mother, but, being younger and more open to new recipes, has also tried the most bizarre combinations—at least for us Japanese: deep-fried soft- shell crab sushi with raw carrots!

When I was a boy, I had never eaten raw fish, and I only knew *maki-zushi* and *chirashi-zushi* with cooked ingre-dients or vegetables. It was only when I came to Tokyo as a young man that I discovered *Edo-mae-zushi*, sushi with raw fish. The first ones I tasted were cheap, only about 10 yen each, but they were so good! I knew I had discovered a fabulous new food, and I've loved it ever since. Shellfish are my favorites, probably because they are light and crunchy and taste of the ocean. I had never asked myself why I like sushi. Because I am Japanese, or simply because, like everybody else, I am touched by their elegance? I know sushi is reassuring. Unlike Western cuisine, made in a kitchen hidden from our eyes, sushi is made in front of you. But more to the point, sushi is a summary of Japanese sensitivity and elegance. Sushi hides its subtlety under a deceptively simple exterior. One cannot guess the hidden depths. One has to know.

Kazuko showed me a kimono, which had belonged to her father. It was a ceremonial kimono, of black silk, absolutely dark and matte. The family emblem, a small white circle with two wisterias, had been embroidered on the back. Very quiet, very dark, very sober. But, the kimono had a magnificent lining. Embroidered with gold and multicolored thread, almost a fresco, with a huge fierce tiger stalking in a forest of tall bamboo. When the person wearing the kimono is just standing still, you can't see the tiger. But, as soon as the person walks, you get a flirting glimpse of the lining, in all its golden magnificence. It's very Japanese. Luxury and elegance are mysterious and furtive, to be glimpsed, not seen.

It is the same with sushi. Sushi is elegant. Sushi is delicious. And, like Kazuko's kimono, sushi hides behind a simple facade. Kazuko has taught me the key to the enigma of sushi. Now, I can decipher it. You, too, with the help of this book, will discover the secrets of sushi. Don't lose a single grain of rice...

Kenzo

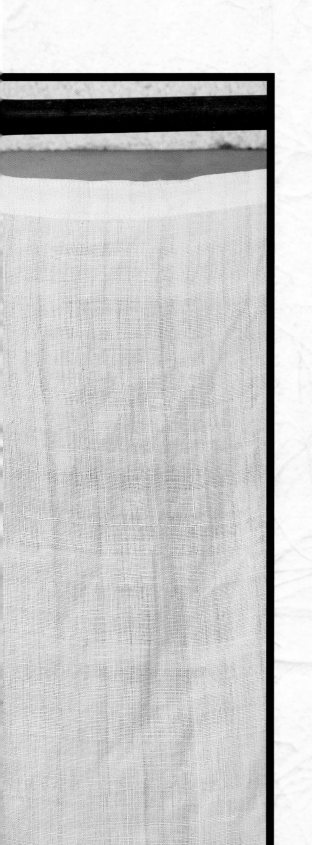

MITATE GENJI HANA-NO-EN UKIYOE BY UTAGAWA KUNISADA

(1786-1864), SIGNED TOYOKUNI III, FAMOUS EDO ARTIST.

THE ENGRAVING IS PART OF A SERIES DEPICTING THE

12 MONTHS OF THE YEAR. HERE, THE MONTH OF APRIL,

A SCENE OF *HANAMI*. A SUSHI PICNIC UNDER CHERRY

BLOSSOMS IN BLOOM. COURTESY PRIVATE COLLECTION.

A PLACE-SETTING AT THE SUSHI COUNTER.

FROM TOP TO BOTTOM: THE SMALL CONTAINER OF

SOY SAUCE, CUP OF TEA, DAMP HAND TOWEL, SMALL

PLATE FOR SOY SAUCE, AND CHOPSTICKS, WRAPPED

IN PAPER WITH THE NAME AND PHONE NUMBER OF

THE RESTAURANT, RESTING ON A *HASHI-OKI*.

A SUSHI PLATTER AT TSURUHACHI

(TOKYO): *TEKKA-MAKI, TORO,*

HIRAME, KOHADA, SEA BREAM,

ANAGO, MIRUGAI, AKAGAI, TAMAGO.

MEMORIES OF SUSHI...

- One of my fondest memories of childhood is coming down with a bad cold. Every year, in February, it never failed. My mother, tucking me up in bed with a cold, damp cloth on my forehead, would run to one of the only two sushi-bars in Paris and bring back a wooden box. After a few tears because I was too hot and my head hurt and my throat ached, and I enjoyed being clucked over, I would open the box. Rectangular and made of thin sheets of soft white wood, it held 8 shrimp sushi, wonderfully symmetrical in two pink and white rows; 6 small red tuna rolls at one end of the box, pretty in circles of red, white, and black; and orange-pink ginger tucked away in one corner behind a green plastic leaf, with a small plastic fish filled with soy sauce. As I opened the box, a wonderfully soft aroma of damp Japanese wood, rice vinegar, *nori*, ginger, and something sweet, which I now know to be sushi rice, would waft out, and despite the stuffy nose that I must have been suffering from at the time, I can still remember it.

- After squirting a drop of soy sauce, I would enjoy the cool sensation of the sushi in my hot, irritated throat. It was a comforting taste: rich and salty enough to be tasted despite my cold, but soothing from the natural sweetness of the rice. Sweet also, from the boiled shrimp and the soft tang of rice vinegar. The red tuna and *nori* (seaweed) brought a bit of the ocean into the sickroom. It tasted of Japan. After two or three sushi, I would lay back on my pillows, totally exhausted but satisfied, and my mother would give me some weak green tea, turn out the light and leave the box on the bedside table. Nowadays, as a responsible adult, I don't cry every time I have a temperature, and don't expect my husband to come rushing back from work to go to the sushi-bar for a take-out box. The closest he gets to sushi for a sore throat is ice cream from the freezer! Growing up is no fun.

CULINARY HAIKU

- What is sushi? A ball of rice with a piece of fish on top? A roll of rice wrapped in seaweed with a bit of fish in the middle? It's a little more than that. Much more.

- Sushi is cuisine, even if it isn't cooked. The rice is carefully chosen, prepared, cooked and seasoned. And the fish... choosing, cutting, preparing the fish is a long story—centuries of history of a people surrounded by poor lands and rich waters. The difference between good and bad sushi is not limited to the freshness of the fish. After all, fresh fish is fresh fish. It's a basic requirement of food in general, without which you can't even think about sushi. There isn't much to say about freshness, especially when you live right by the ocean, you take it for granted.

PLATTER OF *OSHI-ZUSHI* WITH

A BOWL OF SOUP

- Sushi could be said to be symbolic of Japanese culture in general, with its love for simplicity and purity. Pure in the sense that anything superfluous is eliminated. Simple, because it reveals nothing of the tremendous work that goes into its making. Sushi is deceptively simple, at first glance undecorated. As in architecture, literature and poetry, the basis of Japanese culture is to show the essence. Frills are not appreciated.

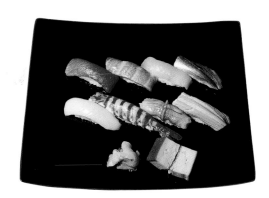

NIGIRI-ZUSHI FOR ONE AT JIRO YOKOHAMA-TEN (YOKOHAMA): RED TUNA, *TORO, HIRAME, KOHADA,* SQUID, SHRIMP, *AKAGAI, ANAGO,* PICKLED GINGER, AND *TAMAGO*

JAPANESE IDENTITY

- To appreciate sushi, you have to forget the tastes and textures that come with Western cuisine. At first glance (or should I say taste?), a sushi of flounder will not be that different from a sushi of sea bream. But, for the Japanese, these two sushi are as different as roast beef and roast pork are for a Westerner.

- Japan is an archipelago of 3,922 islands, with four main islands and 20,500 miles of coastline. Exploiting the ocean was a necessity. Sushi is the result of a long history of life with the sea, during which the Japanese have perfected the art of making the most of fish, even without cooking it.

- In this book, we will tell you all about *Edo-mae-zushi*, sushi of Edo (the old name for Tokyo). It is the best known and probably what comes to mind when you hear the word "sushi." A ball of rice with a slice of raw fish on top, and a row of small black and white rolls. There are many other styles of sushi from different parts of Japan, but none as well known in the world as *Edo-mae-zushi*.

FOUR GREAT CLASSICS

- These are the main types of sushi served in most *sushiya*:
- *Nigiri*: from *nigiru*, to squeeze in the hand. A ball of rice with a slice of fish lightly pressed on top.
- *Maki*: from *maku*, to roll. *Maki-zushi* include all types of sushi rolled in a sheet of *nori*, including *hoso-maki*, a "thin roll" usually containing only one ingredient and cut into six bite-size pieces; *futomaki*, a "thick roll" made up of several ingredients, mostly cooked and sweet; *gunkan-maki*, "battleship maki" a sushi invented in the middle of the last century, named after its shape, a ball of rice topped with a wet or liquid ingredient, held in place with a strip of nori rolled round it horizontally. S*uehiro-maki* or *te-maki*, a relatively new maki, despised by purists, which has a cone shape made from one or several ingredients, rolled by hand.
- *Chirashi-zushi*: from *chirasu*, to scatter. Slices of fish and seafood on a flat bed of rice or, in the east of Japan, rice mixed with vegetables such as shiitake mushrooms, carrots or *kanpyo* (dried gourd), cooked in a sweet sauce, and egg—often served in a lacquered box.
- *Oshi-zushi*: from *osu*, to press or push, a pressed sushi from eastern Japan; seldom made well outside this region.
- There are other types of sushi sold in shops, such as *inari-zushi*, a slice of fried tofu cooked in a sweet sauce stuffed with sushi rice, but these are not served in sushi bars.

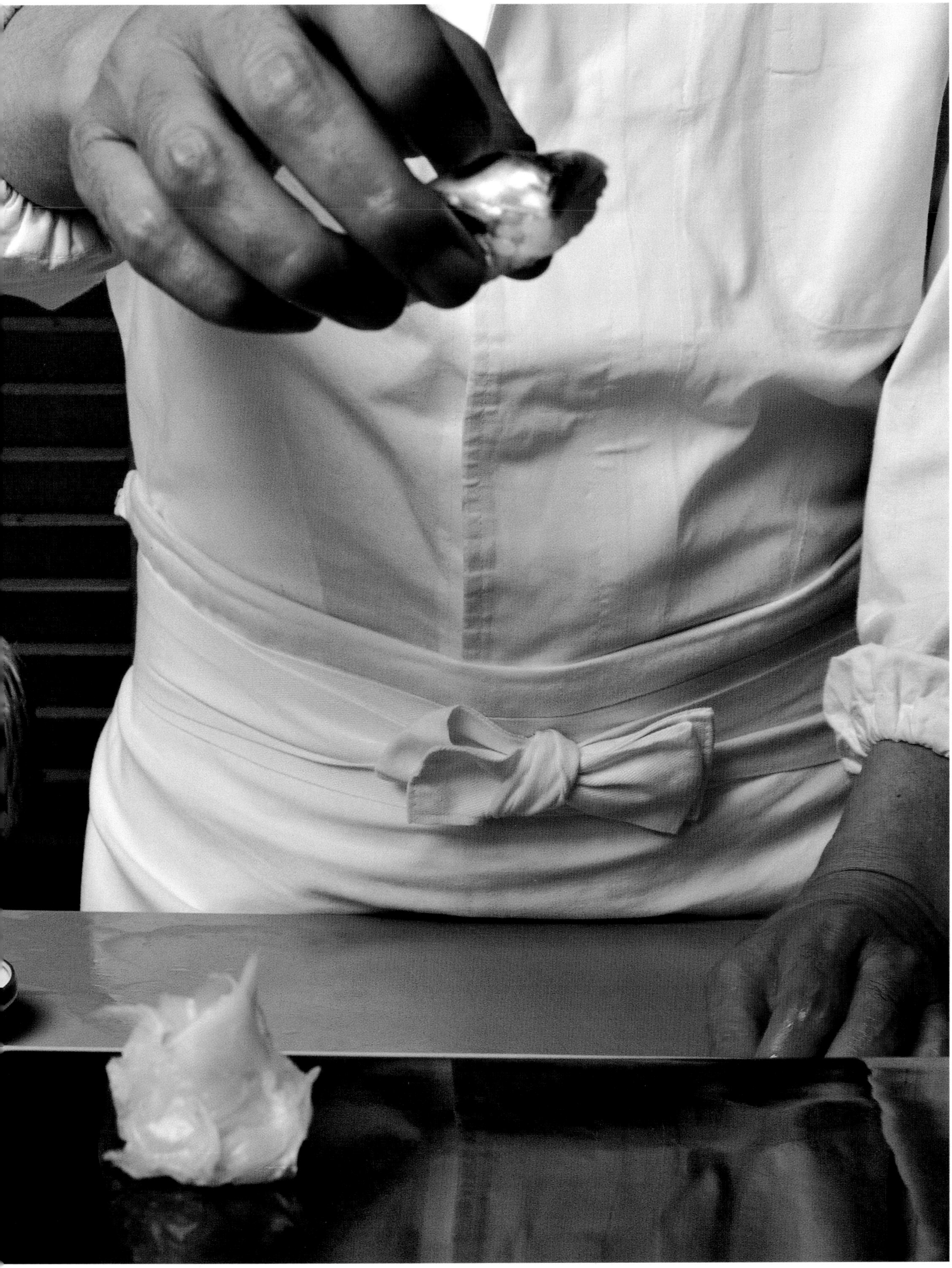

APPEARANCES ARE DECEPTIVE!

- Sushi looks easy: after all, cutting some fish and making a ball of rice can't be that complicated! ... Or is it? First of all, the choice of the fish depends on the season: the same fish may have a refined and subtle taste in spring, but become dry and rough in summer. It may be fresh and light in the fall, but you may prefer it in winter, when it will be heavy with fat that melts deliciously in the mouth. A fish may be best eaten practically alive and very crunchy, whereas another may need a few days to rest and mature, so that its meat will lose a little of it toughness... but not too much.

- Cutting is the most important step in the preparation of fish. A sushiya has his two knives, sharpened and polished, and will never part from them. He cuts the fish in a single slicing movement, the knife inclined at a 45° angle from the cutting board, and never saws the flesh. You can understand how this single movement has to be faultless! Each part of the fish requires a different cut in order to reveal all the secrets, flavors and textures of its flesh.

- If the difference between roasted and boiled meat is obvious, the difference between a slice of raw fish and another slice is not so easily distinguished.

- Last but not least, the rice. Where *sashimi* is sliced raw fish on its own, sushi is sliced raw fish lightly pressed on a ball of vinegared rice. The quality of the sushi depends on the rice: 80 percent of a sushi is rice (look at it sideways and you will see). Any sushiya will tell you: "you can buy the fish, but the rice... that's a different story."
The term *sushiya* is loosely used for both the restaurant or sushi-bar, and the person who makes the sushi. The official term for the sushi-maker is *sushi shokunin* (sushi artisan) and *sushi chorishi* (sushi cook), but they are rarely used in everyday language. In Japan, if you are talking to a sushiya, say *Oyakata* or *Oyaji-san*, which is the traditional way to address the owner or head of a sushi restaurant, and if you are not sure whether he is the chef or not, don't call him anything.

TEN YEARS OF LEARNING

- When I asked the owner and chef of *Jiro*, in Yokohama, who is probably the best living sushiya in Japan, why he only serves once a day, in the evening, and is closed for lunch, he replied: "we could open for lunch too, but the preparation is so long it takes us almost all day just to get ready for the dinner time service."
Admittedly, sushi requires patience and time, even though sushiya are traditionally despised by other Japanese cooks, because they only use two knives, instead of the usual ten used by the traditional Japanese chef, and cannot be called *itamae* (in front of the cutting board), the common term for the Japanese cook.

CHIRASHI AT NONTARO (KYOTO):

SANSHO, LOTUS ROOT, SNOW PEA

PODS, TUNA, SEA BREAM, *TORIGAI*,

SAYORI, SQUID, SHRIMP, *ANAGO*,

HERRING ROE, EGG, *NORI* FLAKES,

SHIITAKE MUSHROOMS, RICE,

VINEGAR, SALT, AND SUGAR.

THE RECIPE OF THE *SU-MESHI*

IS A SECRET.

TAKE-AWAY BOX OF "COOKED"

SUSHI FROM KANDA SHINODAZUSHI

(TOKYO): THREE ROLLS OF *KANPYO*,

TWO *FUTO-MAKI*, THREE *INARI-*

ZUSHI, SWEET AND SALTY FRIED

TOFU STUFFED WITH SUSHI RICE.

BO-ZUSHI OF MARINATED MACKEREL

AT TAKOTAKE. THIS PRESSED SUSHI IS

A SPECIALTY OF OSAKA: A SHEET OF SWEET

KOMBU SEAWEED TOPS THE MACKEREL.

- Cutting techniques are only taught toward the end of the apprenticeship of a sushiya. During the first three years, the apprentice learns to choose, open and clean the fish, cook the ones that need to be cooked, in short, all the basic techniques concerning fish. After three years he will practice forming rice balls—not with rice, such a waste!—but with a piece of damp cloth. Then, he graduates to practicing with soybean scraps, which have a grainy and soft texture that resembles rice. During his fifth year, Oyakata, the Master, will give him a knife and a discreet corner of the counter, recognizing that even though the apprentice is not a real professional, he is still better than nothing. At last, in his seventh year of apprenticeship, he may be allowed to make a few clumsy sushis for some open-minded regular customers. He can then pass the national test to become officially a *sushi chorishi* (sushi cook). After a minimum of ten years, he may deem himself good enough to serve customers himself.

- Sushi artisans have always formed a world apart from the others. They have even developed their own language: *shari* (rice), *gari* (sweet-and-sour pickled ginger), *agari* (tea), *sushi-dane* (the ingredient, often fish, which is placed on the ball of rice).

WHATEVER YOU WANT, WHEN YOU WANT IT

- As opposed to Western cuisine, which follows a rigid order (first course, main course, dessert), sushi is eaten in whatever order you like, as much as you like. In fact, this freedom is what makes it difficult for the uninitiated. Without knowing the names of the fish, their characteristics, their taste and texture, you will often end up choosing the assortment or set menu. But the real connoisseur will not order an assortment served at the table. For one thing, sushi should be eaten at the counter immediately after leaving the hand of the sushiya. And an assortment is by definition contrary to the free spirit of sushi. This is what you should do: look at "today's selection," displayed on small wooden boards on the wall behind the counter, and choose the sushi you want, at the precise moment you want it. If you don't know what to pick, look over the shoulder of your neighbor. If his mackerel looks perfect, the meat firm enough to be pleasant, but also soft enough to melt in your mouth, and if he seems thoroughly satisfied with his choice, just say: "*Oyakata, tsugi wa saba ne*" ("Oyakata, the next one will be mackerel"), to taste the same pleasure. Each person has his or her own rhythm. Sushi is served in pairs, two by two (*nikan*), but you may ask for one only (*ikkan*). If you really don't know what to eat, ask *Oyakata* to make you an *omakase* ("I leave it to you"): "*Oyakata, omakase de onegai shimasu.*" He will serve you the choice fish of the day, in whatever order he thinks will bring out the best of his art.

PLATTER FOR THREE AT TSURUHACHI

(TOKYO). CUCUMBER *MAKI, TORO,*

MIRUGAI, AKAGAI, TEKKA-MAKI,

KOBASHIRA, TAMAGO, ANAGO,

SAYORI, HIRAME, RED TUNA, SQUID,

KOHADA, GINGER.

VEGETABLE SUSHI FROM KYOTO.

LEFT, A *NIGIRI* OF *MENEGI* WITH

A BELT OF *NORI*. CENTER, A *NIGIRI*

OF ALOE VERA WITH A PIECE

OF SALTED DRIED PRUNE.

RIGHT, A *GUNKAN-MAKI* OF *NATTO*

(FERMENTED SOY BEANS).

CHINESE ANCESTORS

- The origins of sushi are lost in the far reaches of history, but, as with numerous elements of Japanese culture, the first traces can be found in China. The first written sign of sushi, a Chinese character still used today in Japan, appears in a dictionary thought to be from the 4th or 3rd century BC. Sushi was at first a method of preserving fish, which was marinated for a long time in a mixture of rice and salt. The fermented rice was discarded, and the fish eaten.

- Sushi is said to have come to Japan during the 8th century. The Japanese started by following the Chinese recipe, but soon after shortened the fermentation process and ended up by eating the rice as well. The amount of rice in the sushi grew with the appearance of *bo-zushi* (sushi rolled in the shape of a thick stick) and *hako-zushi* (sushi pressed in a box). However, the main goal of these sushi was still preservation. To this day, *bo-zushi* from Kyoto, or *hako-zushi* from Osaka are set aside to rest for a time before being eaten, and can be kept for up to 24 hours.

- In a history of sushi going back for more than 2,000 years, *nigiri-zushi* is a comparative newcomer. There are many theories on its origins. The most picturesque story is that of a doctor named Matsumoto, who came to Edo around 1675. Poverty forced him to find alternative sources of income. At the time sushi had to be ordered several days in advance, but Matsumoto invented a sushi that was ready immediately. This "fast-sushi," christened "sushi we don't have to wait for," was a great success and the doctor lived in comfort for the rest of his life!

THE EDO ERA (1603–1867)

- With 850,000 inhabitants in 1700 (London at that time had 500,000 and Paris slightly less), and an area of 27 sq miles, Edo, or the "Door of the Estuary" was the largest city in the world. Lords, monks, merchants, artisans, fishermen, workers, peasants, roaming samurais, and criminals, all gathered to make their fortune, forming an active vibrant urban center and the cradle of Japanese culture as we know it today.

- If Kyoto, in the west—the residence of the Emperor and the Imperial court—was the capital of Japan, Edo was the seat of the Bakufu, the military government of the Tokugawa Shogun, the ultimate power in Japan. Although the Bakufu was a military dictatorship, peace reigned in the archipelago for the first time in history: no more civil wars, no more wars with Korea. Japan closed its doors to foreign influence: Portuguese missionaries were executed; contact with foreigners was forbidden and Japanese Christians were persecuted.

SMALL ASSORTMENT AT SUSHI-ZEN

(*SAPPORO, HOKKAIDO*): SCALLOP,

TUNA, *HOKKIGAI*, PEONY SHRIMP

WITH EGGS, YOUNG SALMON,

SANMA WITH *MENEGI*.

- But the Edo era was 300 years of peace and prosperity for the populace. With the extensive palaces of the aristocracy occupying half of the city, the ordinary people lived in overcrowded conditions, in 3½ sq miles of small two-story houses, with water-wells and lavatories shared by several families. Popular arts prospered (*ukiyoe*), as did theater, dance, music, games, baths, and prostitution. Whole areas of Edo were devoted to the pursuit of pleasure.

19-9

- Edo never slept. The city had a lot of mouths to feed. Innumerable stands flourished: vendors selling bowls of buckwheat noodles, grilled eel, sticky rice balls, fried tempura fish or vegetables and... sushi. At the Kabuki theater, the sumo games, the resting rooms of the public baths or in the brothels, everywhere and all day long, the people of Edo munched on sushi.

YOHEE, A FLAMBOYANT HERO OF SUSHI

- One day, a man known as Yohee the Flamboyant (Hanaya Yohee 1799–1858) appeared in the narrow streets of Edo. According to legend, Yohee, an orphan, started his career at the age of nine as a servant boy in the household of a tax collector and went on to sell rice cakes and antiques. He rented a small house in an overcrowded area of Edo, and every evening until sunrise he walked the streets of the city selling the sushi he had made during the day. By around 1818, he had saved up enough money to open a small sushiya, which soon became so well known that all the aristocracy ordered its sushi there. One of the best-known names of Japanese culinary history, Yoheezushi closed in the 1930s.

- The actual form of *nigiri-zushi*, as well as the now common assortments offering a sushi of each category of ingredient (marinated in vinegar, red and white, cooked, grilled, etc.), are all said to have been invented by Yohee. One and a half centuries after his death, Yohee the Flamboyant is still a major landmark in the history of sushi. A haiku from the Edo era is eloquent on the subject:

Sea bream and flounder

Always the flavor of Yoheezushi

Customers waiting in the shop are

As pressed as nigiri-zushi in a box.

THE TRADITION OF THE SUSHIYA

- At Edo, the major sushi houses, Matsugazushi, Kenukizushi and Yoheezushi, took orders and served in private rooms. Sushi-stands, on the other hand, were portable huts made up of a counter and a roof, transported hanging on a long stick, each end supported on a man's shoulder. In these sushi were made—like hotdogs in New York—fast, cheap and to order. The most popular sushi were made in advance: there were always four or five laid out in a row on the counter. The customers were daily workers, travelers or roaming samurai, who ate quickly and on the spot. Therefore the sushiya had to make as many sushi as possible, as fast as possible.

- Helped by this economic necessity for speed, the ingredients of sushi-stands became less and less elaborate, and were finally served raw. Sushi was soon to become the favorite food of the *Edokko*, "children of Edo," as the inhabitants of Edo were known. That the Bay of Edo was particularly rich in fish also helped. Around 1800, each of the 808 areas of Edo (each area being a block) had one or two sushiya. The *Edokko* disdained the sushi of the aristocracy as being too elaborate and forced the best sushi houses to gradually adopt the sushi of the sushi-stands.

- You can imagine the work of the sushiya, alone behind the counter of his makeshift stand, making sushi, serving tea, counting money, polishing the wood of his shop and his tools. His shop was "full" as soon as he had five customers standing in front of him, with even more customers waiting impatiently behind. Do you know why the teacups of sushi bars today are so big? To save time. With big cups, the sushiya didn't have to pour tea as often. To serve sake would have been totally impossible.

THE DECLINE AND REBIRTH OF SUSHI

- In 1868, the Emperor took back the control of the country from the Bakufu, opened it to foreign trade, moving his court to Edo, which was renamed Tokyo. But fascism, war, and economical crises were soon to darken the sky of the Land of the Rising Sun. The Edo era stays alive in the memory of the Japanese as a decadent but joyful, lively, popular, and creative period.

JAPANESE KNIVES HAVE A SINGLE BEVEL, SHARPENED ONLY ON ONE SIDE OF THE BLADE (RIGHT SIDE FOR A RIGHT HANDED PERSON), THEY ARE RAZOR SHARP, THIN AND INCISIVE, AND CUT THROUGH THE FINE FIBER AND FRAGILE MEAT OF THE FISH WITHOUT BREAKING OR TEARING THEM. THEY ARE HELD AT A 45° ANGLE FROM THE CUTTING BOARD. THE KNIFE IS SO INCISIVE THAT THE CUT IS EFFORTLESS AND PERFECTLY SMOOTH. TO MAKE A SUSHI THAT JUST SLIPS INTO THE MOUTH, THE SURFACE OF THE FISH THAT COMES IN DIRECT CONTACT WITH THE PALATE SHOULD BE AS SMOOTH AS A MIRROR: THIS SIDE OF THE SLICE WAS AGAINST THE UNSHARPENED SIDE OF THE BLADE.

OPPOSITE

KAKINO-HA-ZUSHI OF NARA.

SUSHI OF SALTED MACKEREL AND

SALMON, PRESSED, CUT, AND WRAPPED

IN PERSIMMON LEAVES.

- The structure of the sushi-houses was permanently transformed. Several major establishments were closed: Matsugazushi in 1926, Yoheezushi in 1935, Narutozushi in 1940. In the 1930s, just before World War II, there were only 3,100 sushiya left in Tokyo, with 800 stands. In 1939, new laws controlling public health and hygiene signaled the end of the sushi-stand. World War II, with severe rationing of rice and fish, nearly marked the end of sushi itself. But a providential agreement negotiated between the Tokyo Association of Sushi and the Americans, allowed the customers to bring their rice and exchange it for sushi. This made sushi-houses the first food establishments to open legally, without having to resort to the black market or underground sales. New and readily available ingredients, such as Chinese *mactra* (often called round clam or yellow clam), *tamago* (sweet omelet and *kanpyo* (dried gourd strips) were discovered. The rationing of rice, limiting the number of *nigiri* to ten per person, changed the size of the *nigiri*, which shrank from one and a half mouthfuls to one mouthful.

REVOLVING SUSHI

- With the explosive economic expansion of the post-war period, sushi, the Japanese version of fast food, rapidly became more and more expensive. In the 1970s, the first revolving sushi-bars, *kaiten-zushi* or *mawari-zushi* (literally "turning sushi"), started providing cheap, quick, and easy sushi. These restaurants had a simple, circular, rubber conveyor belt, with the sushiya in the middle, making sushi non-stop, and placing them in small dishes on the belt. The customers sitting around the the belt simply pick up the dish of sushi they fancy, as you would your luggage at the airport. Today, some of these counters have double or even triple layers of conveyor belts, and in some places a machine makes the sushi. The ingredients are more and more varied, some sushi are served with mayonnaise, and why not hamburger sushi too?

PLANET SUSHI

- The original recipe of preserved fermented fish has been discarded with time. It has evolved into the wonderful match of fish and vinegared rice loved throughout the world. Today, sushi has become a symbol of perfect harmony, with a Japanese identity: sea and fish; Asia and rice.

- A true ambassador of Japanese culture, sushi has traveled extensively. Ever since its origins in Edo, it has shown its double nature—a precious gift between the samurai lords, a cheap meal for the manual worker. Even today, sushi is a popular food, but with a prestige enabling it to adorn the best tables. Recent ideas on nutrition as well as the rhythm of life in modern times tend to position it as the food of the 21st century. Luxury or fast food, accompanied by all the virtues of raw fish, it is eaten with the fingers, like a sandwich. And if the sushiya who have emigrated to other countries are holders of a secular tradition, they are adapting with great creativity to local produce. One day, in Detroit, I came upon sushi made of cottage cheese. Surprising certainly... but why not?

Chihiro Masui

NIGIRI OF SHRIMP IN A REVOLVING

SUSHIYA: THE PLATES ARE PILED UP

AND THE COST OF EACH ADDED UP

TO MAKE THE FINAL BILL.

PREVIOUS PAGE

WASABI PLANT

LEFT

JAPONICA KOSHIHIKARI FROM

NAGANO PREFECTURE

rice

Kome (raw rice)/gohan or meshi (cooked rice)/
sumeshi (vinegared rice)

FROM TOP TO BOTTOM

1. **WHOLE RICE**

2. **ROUND-GRAIN HALF POLISHED**

OR HALF MILLED RICE

3. ***KOSHIHIKARI* RICE FOR SUSHI,**

FROM NAGANO

4. **REGULAR *KOSHIHIKARI* RICE,**

FROM NAGANO

5. **LONG-GRAIN RICE FROM THAILAND**

6. **ITALIAN LONG-GRAIN PARBOILED RICE**

7. **BASMATI RICE**

SUSHI IS RICE

- Rice is the main ingredient of sushi. If you look at a *nigiri-zushi* of red tuna from the side, you will see that the slice of fish is only about ¼ inch thick, whereas the ball of rice is just under 1 inch high. Rice is 80 percent of sushi, and the "garnish," usually but not always a product of the sea, is only about 20 percent. Many people think that good sushi is defined by the freshness of the fish. It's not. It's all about rice. Choosing, preparing, cooking and seasoning the rice are so many steps to the perfect sushi.

- *Sumeshi* (literally "vinegared rice") must be perfectly white, with the luster of mother of pearl, and almost translucent. The grain, cooked and seasoned, is oval, round and fleshy—shiny, not as a diamond, but as a pearl. It should have the sweet smell of soft vinegar. When you eat it, the first thing you will notice is the temperature, the same as that of the fish, or slightly hotter, depending on the sushiya. But it should never, never be cold—too much of a shock in the mouth. Neither hard nor compact, the rice ball should be firm, pressed so that the grains of rice stick to each other, but not pressed to the point where these same grains are squashed, damaged and lose their shape. Each grain should be independent enough to be tasted and appreciated individually, round and supple, but must also make a perfect match with its companions to form a ball that does not crumble. I am sure you have already experienced the *nigiri* that crumbled into a shapeless mess the moment it was placed in front of you. As well as the rice ball that was so brutally pressed that you had the unpleasant feeling of having your mouth stuffed with a pasty, indigestible mass. In each case, the verdict is conclusive: low quality rice, badly cooked, badly pressed.

SUBTLE FLAVORS

- The taste of sumeshi is difficult to describe. It is subtly salty, sour and sweet. Each sushiya jealously guards the secret of his seasoning. The harmony between the natural sweetness of the rice, mainly composed of carbohydrates, and the vinegar, salt and sometimes sugar, is the result of skillful dispensing. Acidity is necessary, especially for sushi of fish and seafood, to balance the iodine and fat. Salt brings out the other flavors, sour and sweet, giving the sushi a clean-cut taste. Sugar underlines the softness of the rice, gives it its luster and sweetens the aggressiveness of the vinegar and the salt. A wonderful and complex chemistry!

RICE PADDY IN MAY, NEAR TOKYO.

ACCORDING TO SUSHI AFICIONADOS,

EXTREME TEMPERATURES GIVE THE

BEST RICE: IT IS GROWN IN VALLEYS

SURROUNDED BY HIGH MOUNTAINS,

BATHED IN STRONG SUNLIGHT DURING THE

DAY BUT ENDURING VERY COOL NIGHTS.

PICKING THE RICE

- Sushi rice is meant to accompany a variety of flavors: white fish, refined and delicate; shiny fish, soft and fresh; red tuna, rich in iron; shellfish, packed with iodine; crustaceans, sweet as cake; eel, cooked in a thick sweet sauce. Sushi rice adapts to all these different tastes, emphasizing their strengths, softening their faults.

- But, of course, it can't be just any rice. The best rice, according to the sushiya, is a round-grain rice—the grains should be as small as possible—and "fat." To enable each grain of rice fully to absorb the seasoning, the rice must be cooked with a little less water than rice eaten plain. If the rice is not "fat," meaning that it has no body, no thickness and no luster, it will be too dry. The cooked grains of a "fat" rice have a beautiful round finish: they are nicely swollen and smooth. Too much water makes the rice soggy and pasty. In Japanese, we say that the rice "stands": when the *nigiri* is in your mouth, the grains, until then united in a single ball, separate to enfold the fish and form a perfect match.

- Two species of rice are most valued for sushi: *koshihikari* and *sasanishiki*. Relatively new, they have only been grown since the mid-1950s. Well balanced in starch, with a delicate flavor, they quiclky became immediate favorites on the Japanese market. Since the 1980s, numerous hybrids of *koshihikari* have appeared on the market: *hitomebore* (love at first sight), *akitakomachi* (the belle of Akita), *hinohikari* (light of day), *hoshinoyume* (the dream of the stars), *haenuki*, to name but a few. But if the two great classics of Japanese rice are cultivated everywhere in the country, their taste varies from one region to another, from one rice paddy to its neighbor. The flavor of rice, as with that of wine, is greatly influenced by the region of production, weather and, of course, the skill of the rice farmer.

RICE CULTURE, MORE THAN A CULTURE

- If you take a walk in the Japanese countryside, you will see many small rice paddies, with farmers bent in the water-filled fields, stretching their backs from time to time in a familiar gesture. Nowadays, basketball caps with a towel to protect the back of the neck from the sun have replaced the traditional pointed bamboo hats. But rice farming in Japan has not embraced the new technologies used in the United States, the fields in this narrow country being too small for effective mechanization.

- Rice farming is conducted more or less as it was by our ancestors. The farmer prepares the grains in March, plants them in April. He watches over the little green shoots and waters them regularly. In May, he floods his field, twice, to mix the soil thoroughly with the water. Once the field is ready, he will replant the shoots in neat rows. It is tough, back-breaking work. In June comes the rainy season, with heavy, hot, and continuing rains. The air is almost wet with humidity, which may reach 98 percent. In July, the rice paddy must be aired so that the roots can breathe, giving it a striped look. The hot weather in August is the most determining factor for a good crop. The temperature must not drop below 62°F for more than 10 hours, otherwise the rice plants will be ruined and die. If the weather holds, the rice farmer drains the field in September. The plants are heavy with grain. In a few weeks the grain will become golden. The rice is ripe—it is time for the harvest.

- Harvest has always been celebrated by offerings to the Shinto gods of rice and harvest, and by feasts, at which generous amounts of sake are consumed. According to Shinto beliefs, the Emperor of Japan is the incarnation of *Ninigo-no Mikoto*, the spirit of ripe rice.

- If today, few Japanese believe in this legend, no one will deny the cultural and historical importance of rice. During the Middle Ages, rice was used for the payment of taxes, and the fortune of an individual was calculated by the amount of rice grown on his lands. In Japan, rice is the pillar of life: we eat it, drink it, make vinegar, cakes, and alcohol with it. It marks the cycle of the seasons, the annual rebirth and prosperity. It is an essential player in all celebrations: the New Year is greeted with cakes of sticky rice, a birth or a wedding is feasted with rice reddened with red beans.

A PRECIOUS FOOD

- Rice is a major food crop for more than half of the inhabitants of our planet (155–220 lb eaten every year per inhabitant of Asia, 13 lb only for Europe and the United States). In several Asian tongues "rice" is synonymous to "meal." Instead of calling out "dinner's ready," a Japanese mother will say "Here's the rice!" (*gohan desuyo!*), even if today's dinner is steak with French fries.

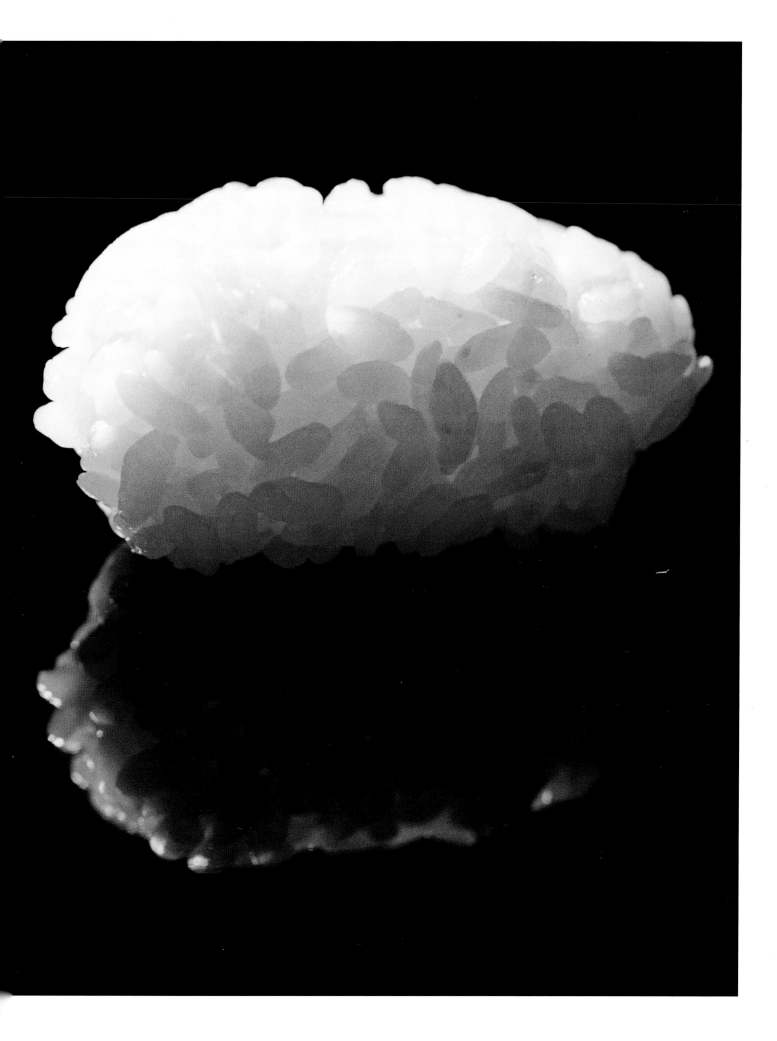

- In Japan, we never forget that a grain of rice may grow into 10 or 15 stalks, each stalk ending in 10 or 15 panicles, each panicle giving a hundred spikelets, each spikelet producing a grain of rice. This is why the stern father who inspects rice bowls at the end of the meal will scold his children by saying: "Do you know how much rice you are wasting? One grain thrown away is 1,000 wasted." It is considered very bad manners to leave even a grain of rice stuck to your bowl.

- The origins of rice are still unknown, and have been a subject of debate for a long time. Archeological studies have placed the cradle of rice culture in Southeast Asia. Rice was already a domestic crop in China in 5000 BC. From there, it is thought to have traveled to Northern Thailand, Cambodia, Vietnam, Southern India. It is from this area that *Japonica* rice (rice grown in temperate climates) and *Indica* (rice grown in tropical climates) extended to the other Asian countries: Korea, Japan, Myanmar (formerly Burma), Pakistan, Sri Lanka, the Philippines, Indonesia... Rice rapidly became a staple in all of Asia. Hindu and Buddhist writings constantly refer to it, and both religions use it as a sacred offering. It is said that the culture of rice by irrigation was developed in China. If rice does not need a lot of water to grow, a large amount of water increases its crop. It is from this water that rice gets its mineral elements. Rice needs a temperature above 68°F for 3 months.

- The types of rice that originated from Asia, known as *Oryza sativa*, include thousands of varieties, grouped into two major families. *Indica* rice is long-grained, thin, and breaks easily. Cooked, it is light, fluffy and does not stick. It is well adapted to dishes such as pilafs, curries, and fried rice and is grown in India, Thailand, and the United States. It is the rice preferred by most Asian and Middle-Eastern populations. *Japonica* rice, however, the only rice that can be used for sushi, has a moist and sticky texture. It is mainly eaten in China, Japan, Korea, Australia and Italy.

ROUND, WHITE AND "NAKED"

- Rice must be shorn of its inedible outer husk. Rice only shorn of its husk is brown rice or whole rice, weighs 80 percent of its initial weight, and retains its bran, which contains a lot of minerals and vitamins. White rice is rice from which the bran has been completely discarded by polishing on metallic graters: it contains fewer nutritional elements and fibers, but is more easily and completely digested.

- If you want to make sushi, never use long-grained rice that doesn't absorb the seasoning of vinegar. Perfumed rice (basmati or Thai) are not compatible with Japanese cuisine: their flavors are too strong and destroy the delicate flavors of sushi. In Japan, we prefer rice to be as little perfumed as possible, "naked," in order to match it with a range of very subtle flavors. Outside of Japan, *koshihikari* grown in California, and certain Italian and Spanish round-grained rice make a good match with Japanese cuisine, including sushi.

RICE IN AUGUST, A MONTH BEFORE HARVEST. IT'S THE MOST IMPORTANT TIME—THE RICE MATURES. IT IS VERY HOT: IF THE TEMPERATURE DROPS BELOW 62°F FOR MORE THAN TEN HOURS, THE RICE WILL SUFFER AND POSSIBLY DIE.

Su/vinegar;
Komesu/rice vinegar

WATERCOLOR BY AN UNKNOWN ARTIST

AT THE END OF THE 19TH OR BEGINNING

OF THE 20TH CENTURY, DEPICTING THE

VARIOUS STEPS OF VINEGAR PRODUCTION

(COURTESY MUSEUM OF VINEGAR,

SUNOSATO HAKUBUTSUKAN).

FROM RIGHT TO LEFT, TOP TO BOTTOM

1. 3-YEAR FERMENTATION OF SAKE

SCRAPS DURING THE EDO ERA.

2. ADDING WATER. 3. PRESSING WITH

LINEN CLOTHS. 4. HEATING TO

FERMENTATION TEMPERATURE.

5. ADDING THE HOT LIQUID INTO

VINEGAR FROM THE PRECEDING

FERMENTATION. 6. MATURING FOR

2 TO 3 MONTHS. 7. FILTERING.

8. "BOTTLING" INTO BARRELS.

ON HOT COALS

- Edo, 200 years ago. Taro the Carpenter is running. Running, running, running. Running between the tiny neighborhood houses of wood and paper. His sandals slap the earth, making clouds of dust billow in the air. He bumps into a group of children playing in the street, who stare after him indignantly as he runs, coming to a sudden stop in front of a house, slams open the sliding door, rushes into the sour-smelling shop and shouts: "Give me some vinegar! Quickly! Quickly!" At this cry of "vinegar," the whole neighborhood knows that Taro's wife is giving birth. His first-born! At last! For such a momentous occasion, the mistress of the house comes to attend to him in person. She comes from the back of the shop, smoothing the sleeves of her kimono. Taro is hopping impatiently from one foot to the other. Mistress Vinegar hands him a bottle of good vinegar, with a comforting smile: "It's for your wife? Don't worry, everything will be fine. Make a good fire with nice red coals. Don't forget to put a thick piece of cloth between her teeth, so she doesn't bite her tongue!" Some time later, the cries of the newborn echo in the air of Edo. The people exchange knowing smiles, relieved that all is well.

- It was the custom in old times to pour vinegar on hot coals to let the woman giving birth breath in the acidic vapors, which were believed to ease the pain. Vinegar was not only a seasoning, but also used as a medicine to relieve fainting; as a disinfectant; a stimulant for the appetite on very hot summer days; a food preservative, and many other things. Today, we know that it also aids digestion, helps with intestinal problems and the absorption of calcium.

- Vinegar is 90–95 percent water, with practically no calories (2 calories per tablespoonful) no fat, very little protein, carbohydrates and vitamins, but its high mineral content helps strengthen bones and muscle.

A VERY OLD SEASONING

- Vinegar is made from the fermentation of alcohol, and is said to be the second oldest seasoning known to man after salt. It whitens or lightens the color of vegetables and breaks down oil, which is why vinegar is almost universally used for salad dressings. All the alcohols in the world have probably been used to make it: not only wine, cider, palm wine, sake, but also malt, sugar cane, dates, bananas and coconut milk.

- Vinegar came to Japan from China during the 5th century, and quickly adapted to local products. Japanese vinegars are made from rice, whole rice, and sake. The Japanese character used to write vinegar 酢 uses the same radical as that of sake 酒. Refreshingly tonic, vinegar plays a discreet but essential role in Japanese cuisine. It gives marinated ginger a pleasantly pinkish hue, and is absolutely essential in sushi.

LABEL OF A BOTTLE OF VINEGAR,

ENTIRELY MADE FROM SAKE SCRAPS:

MITSUBAN YAMABUKI JUN SAKE

KASUZU, 4.5 PERCENT ACIDITY.

RED VINEGAR AND WHITE VINEGAR.

THESE TWO VERY DIFFERENT VINEGARS

ARE USED TO SEASON SUSHI RICE,

DEPENDING ON THE SUSHIYA.

BOTTLE OF CHIDORI-ZU (KYOTO)

4.2 PERCENT ACIDITY

- Used as a preservative for the first sushi, vinegar took on a much more prominent role with the arrival of *nigiri*. A bridge between the taste of fish and rice, it accompanies both to make a perfect match. I have often heard my Western friends exclaim: "It's amazing! I hate fish, but I love sushi!" Nothing surprising to that: vinegar neutralizes tri-methylamine, a molecule responsible for the unpleasant smell of fish.

- Shiny fish (mackerel, jack mackerel, *kohada*) must be salted first to break down a protein (myocin) that hardens meat soaked directly in vinegar, making it dry and stringy. This technique of "cooking" without fire demands skill and knowledge, so that the "time of salt" and the "time of vinegar" is perfectly balanced—the fish should not be too salty nor too sour—to fully open the flavors of the fish. The Ancients had mastered these techniques even though they had no knowledge of biochemistry!

WHITE AND CLEAR, RED AND FULL-BODIED

- The most common vinegar in Japan, and often used by sushiya, is white rice vinegar. In fact, it is not white, but perfectly clear. It has an acidic taste, with no particular aroma or flavor. Fermentation of rice into sake takes about 2 weeks. Another 2 weeks will turn the sake into vinegar. While the level of acidity of vinegars produced around the world is generally between 4 and 8 percent (7 percent for Xeres vinegar, 6 percent for balsamico vinegar), Japanese rice vinegar has only 4.2 percent. It is increasingly used in the West for the seasoning of salads and vegetables, since its mildness allows the seasoning of vegetables without adding oil.

- Red vinegar is traditional vinegar made from fermented sake mash (rice scraps left over after being pressed for sake). It was first made at the beginning of the 19th century, in the village of Handa in the Chita peninsula, by a vinegar-maker named Matazaemon. Of a beautiful deep dark red, it has a complex flavor, sweet but cutting, sturdy and clear, and a sharp, stinging aroma. It takes longer to make than white vinegar: fermented for one month, it is aged for 2 to 3 years. To make red vinegar, the sake mash must be of good quality and be of high alcohol content. The quality of the water is also of great importance, since it determines the action of the bacteria and fermentation, thus defining the taste and aroma of the vinegar. Sushiya who favor taste over color use this red vinegar, which gives a faint reddish tinge to the rice.

soy sauce

shoyu

WITHOUT LOSING A SINGLE GRAIN OF RICE

- To eat sushi with elegance is every sushi lover's dream. Here's the trick: pour a small amount of soy sauce into the little sauce dish, hold the *nigiri* between thumb, forefinger and middle finger, turn it upside down and delicately dip a tip of the slice of fish into the soy sauce. Do not dip the rice; it will instantly absorb the soy, become unstuck and crumble, and you will have an ugly puddle with depressingly untidy white grains in your pretty little saucer.

- If you taste soy sauce by itself, you will only find it salty. But if you pour a few drops on fish, you will discover its full flavor, salty and sweet, with a smoky tangy aroma. A sushi without soy sauce is still sushi, but is somewhat flat. In fact, soy sauce is not really a sauce, but more of a flavoring, since it is used in small quantities to season a dish or a food.

THE PATHS OF WISDOM LEAD TO EXQUISITE DISCOVERIES

- It all started with a Buddhist monk, Kakushin, who traveled to China around 1250, on a quest for wisdom. No one knows whether he found it, but when he came back home four years later, he brought in his packs something which was to take a permanent place in the everyday life of the Japanese: *miso*, a paste made of fermented soy beans. One day when Kakushin was showing his fellow Japanese how to make miso, he found a dark liquid in the bottom of the jar. Curious, no doubt, and greedy, certainly, he tasted it and found it delicious. He had just discovered *tamari* (from the verb *tamaru*, to accumulate).

- Over time, the Japanese tried different recipes. Starting from tamari, made only of soybeans, they discovered *shoyu*, first mixing rice and soy, then wheat and soy. *Shoyu* was produced originally in Osaka and transported to Edo in barrels. The *shoyu* of the west was light, refined and subtle. But the inhabitants of Edo soon learned to prefer the *shoyu* of the east, *koikuchi shoyu*, black, thick and stronger than its western counterpart.

- They say that the first Europeans who sailed into Japan during the 16th century were fascinated by this extraordinary condiment. But a few decades later, the Tokugawa Shoguns were to close Japan to all outside influence. Only a few Dutch merchants were allowed to trade, once a year, with a single boat anchored in the port of Nagasaki. These merchants loaded their boat with *shoyu*, silk and tea, and sold them at exorbitant prices in Europe. Louis XIV, the Sun King of France, had a chef who used *shoyu* to delicately season meat dishes for his sovereign!

INGREDIENTS OF SOY SAUCE:

SOY, WHEAT, AND SALT.

T
H
E

I
N
G
R
E
D
I
E
N
T
S

THE FERMENTATION OF *MOROMI*

SOY BEANS ARE STEAMED.

THE WHEAT IS ROASTED AND CRUSHED.

A RICE-BASED FERMENT IS ADDED.

THE MIXTURE RESTS AT 90°F

AND CLOSE TO 100 PERCENT

HUMIDITY FOR THREE DAYS.

WATER AND SALT ARE ADDED.

THE MIXTURE OBTAINED IS THE *MOROMI*.

AT ONE MONTH, THE FERMENTATION

OF *MOROMI* HAS STARTED BUT IT STILL

RETAINS A LIGHT COLOR.

AT THREE MONTHS, THE SOY BEANS

LOSE THEIR SHAPE.

AT SIX MONTHS, THE *MOROMI* IS READY

TO BE PRESSED AND BE TURNED

INTO *SHOYU*

SHOYU IS POURED INTO A SPECIAL

TASTING CUP TO EVALUATE ITS QUALITY.

THE COLOR IS THE MOST IMPORTANT

FACTOR. IT SHOULD BE A BEAUTIFUL

PURPLE-BROWN.

LABEL OF A KIKKOMAN BRAND BOTTLE

OF *SHOYU*.

SOY OR NOT SOY?

- Soya bean (*Glycine max*) is a legume cultivated since the 11th century BC in wheat-growing areas of the world. Asians did not drink animal milk, and soy, which yielded a white liquid when soaked in water, was known as the "cow of China." Today, soy is everywhere in Japanese food: miso, shoyu, soy flour, tofu, yuba (soy sheets), kinako (soy flour used in cakes), soy sprouts, grilled soy, soy oil, and tonyu (soy milk).

ASIAN NUANCES

- Soy sauce is made from soya bean and wheat. But each Asian country has its own recipe. In China, it is fragrant and thicker because the quantity used is different and the aging process longer (18 to 24 months as opposed to 4 to 6 months in Japan). Indonesian soy sauce is thick and sweet. Korean, Vietnamese and Tibetan soy sauces all have different characteristics. Today, the best-known soy sauce in the world, sold under the Kikkoman label, is the Japanese version. But despite the overwhelming presence of the Kikkoman brand, there are still 1,600 producers in Japan, each making his or her own *shoyu*, adapted to the tastes and preferences of each region. An amazing range of flavors.

- A good *shoyu* has a smoky aroma, reminiscent of roasted nuts, and a salty taste with a background of delicate sweetness, like a light caramel. These qualities evaporate very rapidly at contact with air and heat, which is why you should always keep *shoyu* in an airtight container, stored in the refrigerator, and transfer small quantities as required for the table or for cooking. Be careful, since the "use by" date on the container does not take into account the date at which you open it. Once the bottle is opened, it should be kept in the refrigerator and used as soon as possible if you don't want to find yourself with a salty tasteless liquid.

JAPANESE VARIATIONS

- There are many different types of Japanese *shoyu*:
- *Koikuchi*: black *shoyu*. 82.5 percent of total *shoyu* production in Japan. By far the best-known *shoyu* in the world, it originally came from Edo, and is now available everywhere in Japan. It is made from soy, wheat and salt.
- *Usukuchi*: light *shoyu*. 14.5 percent of total production. This *shoyu* has a higher salt content and is fermented longer, giving it a lighter color. Mainly used in Western Japan, around Kyoto and Osaka, for cooking, since it does not darken the food.
- *Tamari*: the ancestor of *shoyu*. 1.6 percent of total production. Very concentrated and black, it contains little or no wheat. Often used with sashimi.
- *Sashikomi*: *shoyu* fermented twice. Mainly used in the Osaka region.
- *Shiro*: white *shoyu*. Contains more wheat and salted water than the others.

A ROOM OF NATURAL FERMENTATION,

IN WOOD, AT KIKKOMAN. BUILT IN 1939

FOR THE FERMENTATION OF *SHOYU*

DESTINED FOR THE IMPERIAL FAMILY.

TODAY, PART OF THE *SHOYU* PRODUCED

HERE IS BOUGHT BY THE IMPERIAL

FAMILY, THE REMAINDER IS SOLD ON

THE OPEN MARKET.

nori

Porphyra tenera

A TENDER HEARTED DOMESTIC TYRANT

- My grandfather was a Japanese of the old school where men do not belong in the kitchen: he wouldn't even get a glass of water for himself. Every day at mealtimes, he would come and sit at the table, and if my grandmother hadn't brought him a full plate and a bowl of rice within the next second, he would rage and threaten divorce. After a few decades of marriage, nobody took him seriously, but we were all very quiet and lowered our heads until the storm had passed. Then, he would finish his meal in about three minutes and leave the room, even though the rest of us had only just picked up our chopsticks. Of course, I have never seen him clear the table, let alone heat water for his tea.

- There was one exception though—when I paid my annual visit to my grandparents. When I arrived, it was always the same: he would barge into the kitchen to make *futomaki*, flustering my grandmother who was quietly sitting drinking tea. Since he never cooked, he would just stand in front of the cutting board and shout: "Rice! Nori! Where are the mushrooms? Why are you are so slow?" My poor grandmother had to rush around for the ingredients, which caused a lot more work than usual. But my grandfather had to make *futomaki* with his own hands, for his favorite granddaughter who had come so far, from Paris, France!

- Mushrooms, spinach, *soboro, tamago, kanpyo,* sushi rice, and *nori* were rolled into a thick roll, and cut into 8 thick slices. After such an intense operation, I would eat my own *futomaki*, or "thick roll," all by myself. I have heard that my grandfather used to make my mother *futomaki* when she was a child, for her school outings, more than sixty years ago. And his mother probably made him *futomaki* when he had a school outing, or, who knows, perhaps his father did too.

DELICIOUS LITTLE PACKAGES

- People all over our planet have, at some point of their culinary history, rolled food in an edible envelope: vine leaves in Greece, spring rolls in Vietnam, tortillas in Mexico, crêpes in France, briks in North Africa, and so on. It is easy to take away and eat, as well as pretty, delicious, and filling. And in Japan we have the *maki*, a sushi rolled in *nori*.

- *Nori* is seaweed; coastal people have often eaten seaweed, the vegetables of the sea. There are 25,000 species of seaweed in the world but only 40 or 50 are edible. Thanks to sushi, the best known of all these species is *nori*. It is an everyday food in Japan: you will find it in every kitchen, every day. Children munch it as a snack, plain or rolled around cheese, for example.

ROUGH SIDE OF A SHEET OF *NORI* CUT IN TWO. IT'S ON THIS SIDE THAT THE RICE IS SPREAD. THE SMOOTH SIDE IS THE ONE THAT COMES IN CONTACT WITH THE MOUTH.

A PACKET OF TOP QUALITY NORI,

IN A PARCEL BEARING THE

YAMAMOTO SHIIRE LABEL

- *Maki* is an ideal harmony between the almost acidic flavor of red tuna, the mild twinge of *wasabi*, the soft sweetness of rice seasoned with rice vinegar, and a good *nori* of deep green, purple and blue, crunchy under the teeth, tightly rolled and yet without crushing a single grain of rice.

NORI THE PRIMITIVE PLANT

- We don't know who was the first to conceive the strange notion of eating weeds picked in the sea, chopped, shaped into sheets and dried. In 718, *nori* is mentioned in the *Taiho Code* (the first Japanese text of law) as a taxable produce. At the time it was not yet farmed: fishermen went to gather it from the ocean in pairs—the first man would row the small boat, the second pluck the weed. *Nori* was a rare luxury and had a prominent place on the Imperial table. *Nori* cultivation was developed during the Edo era. Today, it is a multi-million dollar industry that has expanded to all the coastal regions of Japan.
- The process is complex, since *nori*, as all seaweed, is a *thallus*, one of the first plants to have existed on earth. It has no root, no stalk, no leaf, and no vascular system. The grains are planted in seashells and grow into filaments. These filaments are replanted on nets, where the plant continues to grow. Once the seaweed is picked, it is chopped and shaped into rectangular sheets and set to dry in processing centers. Raw *nori* is purple or red and turns into a dark green and black color when dried. Each sheet weighs about 3 grams. Its price may vary from 15 yen to 1500 yen per sheet, depending on the region of production, the color, aroma, and taste. The upper side of the sheet is smooth, and is the outer side of the *maki*, where it comes in direct contact with the mouth. The inside of the *maki* is the rough side of the *nori*, where the rice adheres well, and is not as pleasant on the palate.

GOOD TO EAT, GOOD FOR HEALTH

- *Nori* has a mild smoky flavor and a very faint aroma of iodine. It is sold dried, roasted, plain, or seasoned. It should always be lightly grilled before use: take two sheets and put them together, smooth side on the inside, and wave them several times over an electric grill. A good roasted *nori* takes on a brilliant green color, tinged with purple, and will be very crunchy.
- Like soy, *nori* contains a lot of vegetable protein: 10 times more vitamin A than butter, 7 times more vitamin B2 than egg, more calcium than milk, more vitamin C than many fruits and vegetables, as well as vitamin E. Numerous studies have shown the cancer-fighting properties of edible seaweed, especially *nori*, with its fiber, high beta carotene content, and high-quality essential fatty acids.
- Choose your *nori* well: the mineral and trace element content of a high-quality nori will be twice that of a low-grade nori, and it will also be much more tasty!

A GRATED *WASABI* ROOT.

THE GRATER IS MADE OF SHARKSKIN.

"FIELDS" OF *WASABI* IN MAY, AT SHIZUOKA.

WASABI IS GROWN AT AN ELEVATION OF

985–1,312 FEET, IN TERRACED FIELDS

BATHED IN CLEAR WATER FROM A MOUNTAIN

SOURCE, AND AT A TEMPERATURE OF

50–60°F. IT NEEDS 5 TO 6 TIMES MORE

OXYGEN THAN MOST OTHER PLANTS.

wasabi

Wasabia japonica matsumu

GREEN, PIQUANT AND FRESH

- *Wasabi* is a vivacious plant of the cruciferous family, indigenous to Japan. It needs perfectly clear flowing water (mountain sources) and does not do well in temperatures higher than 68°F.

- Everything is edible. The root, the small, white flowers, the leaves, and the stalk. But only the root is used as a condiment. Wrapped in wet newspaper, it can be stored for one month in the refrigerator. *Wasabi*, grated in a circular motion, becomes a slightly sticky bright green paste. The best grater is the traditional sharkskin grater. *Wasabi* is very pungent immediately after being grated, but its heat decreases with time. It is set to rest for a while in a covered container in order to let it breathe and lose its bitterness.

- Often compared to horseradish, *wasabi* is milder and less bitter. It allies pungency, sweetness, freshness, with an aroma close to that of fresh horseradish. This harmony of aromas makes it a perfect match for raw fish. It has been known and mentioned in Japanese literature since the 8th century, but cultivated only since the beginning of the 17th century and the Edo era, when it was used as an antiseptic for fish. Two centuries later, it had become appreciated for its taste and was a staple in Japanese cuisine. We know today that *wasabi* fights bacteria and parasites.

THE TRUTH, THE LIE, THE POWDER AND THE PASTE

- A fragile plant, difficult to grow (two years between planting and harvest) and needing a lot of care, real Japanese *wasabi* has always been expensive. Most Japanese *wasabi* goes directly to restaurants and sushiya. The *wasabi* roots sold in supermarkets in Japan are imported from China, Korea, Indonesia and Thailand.

- How to recognize real *wasabi*? It is mild, almost sweet. Supple and smooth on the tongue, it leaves a refreshing grass-like green taste in the mouth. It is not "spicy" like red pepper but pleasantly pungent, and does not sting the nose aggressively.

- Faced with an increase of demand, powdered *wasabi* was invented at the beginning of the 20th century, followed in the 1960s by *wasabi* paste sold in tubes. At first, real Japanese *wasabi* processed into a dry powder was used, but it was soon substituted by horseradish. Powdered *wasabi* has to be mixed with a little cold water until it takes on a green pasty texture. Be careful: the more you mix, the more pungent it gets. *Wasabi* paste is ready to use and needs to be kept in the refrigerator after opening. These substitute *wasabi* have practically no flavor and have a much stronger sting than the "real" thing.

ginger

Zingiber officinalis—Shoga

EASY RECIPE FOR *GARI*

8 OZ FRESH GINGER

2 TSP SALT

1 CUP RICE VINEGAR

5–5½ TBSP SUGAR

4 TBSP WATER

PEEL AND THINLY SLICE THE GINGER.

SPRINKLE WITH THE SALT AND SET

ASIDE FOR 1 TO 2 HOURS. COMBINE

THE VINEGAR, SUGAR, AND WATER IN

A PAN, HEAT GENTLY UNTIL THE SUGAR

HAS MELTED. SQUEEZE OUT THE

GINGER WITH YOUR HANDS AND DROP

INTO BOILING WATER FOR 2 MINUTES

(LESS IF YOU PREFER A MORE PUNGENT

FLAVOR). STRAIN AND ADD IT, HOT,

TO THE VINEGAR MIXTURE, LET IT COOL,

AND IT'S READY! THIS WILL KEEP FOR

ABOUT 3 WEEKS IN THE REFRIGERATOR,

TIGHTLY-PACKED IN A CONTAINER.

SUSHI'S BEST FRIEND

- Ginger is a tuberous rhizome, cultivated in tropical countries and certain temperate climates. Japanese ginger, now a rarity even in Japan, is pink, whereas ginger from the Asian continent is yellow. Many sushiya use artificially colored ginger imported from China or Taiwan.

- Ginger always comes with sushi. You see a small pile of pale pink and yellow in a corner of the platter or directly on the counter. Called *gari* in the sushi lingo, ginger pickled in rice vinegar, salt, and sugar refreshes the mouth after fish, stimulates the appetite or "rinses" the mouth and prepares it for new flavors to come.

- *Shoga,* or raw ginger, is often grated to accompany shiny fish, especially Japanese jack mackerel or scad, commonly referred to as horse mackerel. Slightly pungent with a long-lasting pointed aroma, it glosses over the metallic aftertaste of shiny fish.

- New ginger, *shin-shoga*, is gathered in March. It is white, tender with a soft and refined aroma. It does not need to be peeled. It may be kept for a year, but a thin skin will start to grow over it around September, thicken in October, and turn yellow or brown. This skin should be peeled. At this stage, the aroma becomes more aggressive, the flavor, spicy and hot.

A STIMULANT AND AN APHRODISIAC

- Lauded in ancient Chinese and Indian texts for its medicinal attributes, also appreciated by the Greeks and the Romans, ginger arrived in Western Europe towards the end of the 12th century, where, at first, it was much sought after. But it was soon to be neglected and forgotten. It has always been extensively used in Asian kitchens. Today in Japan, ginger-flavored chocolate, sherbet, and sweets are very popular.

- A stimulant, antiseptic, diuretic, and aphrodisiac, ginger promotes digestion and calms morning sickness during pregnancy. Whenever I feel a cold coming, I take a whole root of ginger, roughly chopped, and let it steep in hot water on very low heat. I add some lemon juice and honey just before drinking the strained liquid. Try it: it is not only delicious, but will really warm you up. There is nothing better for a stuffy nose.

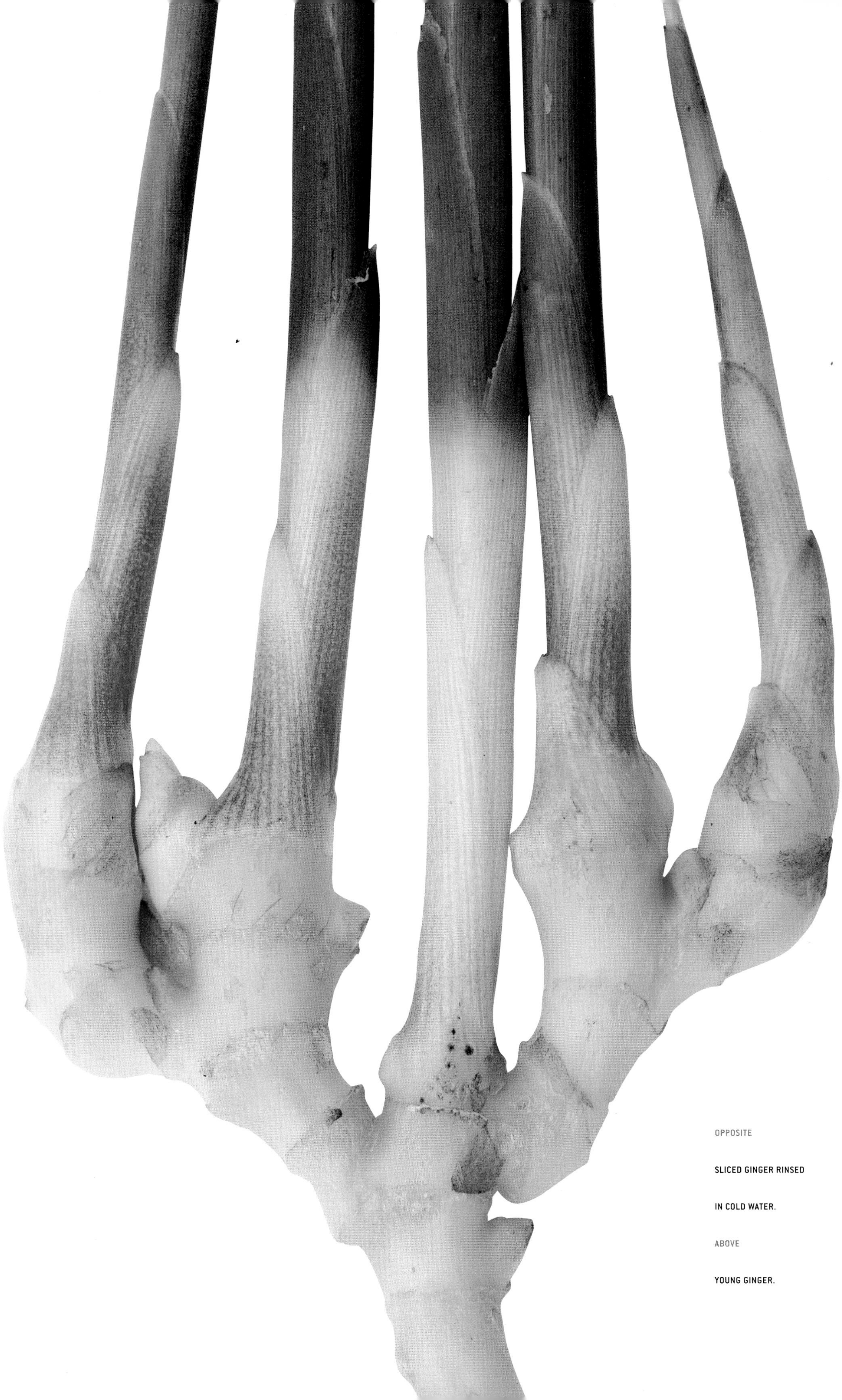

OPPOSITE

SLICED GINGER RINSED

IN COLD WATER.

ABOVE

YOUNG GINGER.

INTRODUCTION
THE INGREDIENTS

THE FISH MARKET

THE SUSHI
THE RECIPES
VOYAGE TO THE LAND OF SUSHI
TIPS

Tsukiji. The biggest fish market in the world.

A city within a city, of busy crossings, avenues and paved alleys.

Where night is day. An entire city covered with a single roof.

Forever wet, puddles of water glistening under fluorescent lights

and naked light bulbs. Tsukiji: an area of 276,080 sq yards;

2,344 tons of produce from the sea sold each day; 15,000

rubber-booted workers, 21 sanitary inspectors, 17,000 trucks

and numberless scooters, mechanical and manual trolleys.

THE BIGGEST TUNA IN THE HISTORY OF TSUKIJI WEIGHED 1096 LB. THE MOST EXPENSIVE WAS SOLD AT 100,000 YEN PER KILO, AND WEIGHED 445 LB.

5:45 A.M. THE BUYERS AND MIDDLEMEN RESPOND WITH LIGHTENING SPEED TO THE SELLER'S LOUD CONTINUING JUMBLE OF WORDS—SO FAST THE LAYMAN ONLY CATCHES A WORD HERE AND THERE—BY BIDDING WITH THE FINGERS OF ONE HAND.

8:00 A.M. QUIET AT LAST. THE RETAILERS HAVE GONE TO EAT AT ONE OF THE FIFTY EATING PLACES OF TSUKIJI. AT 10:00 A.M., EVERYBODY IS ALREADY CLEANING, WASHING, DISINFECTING, TAKING ORDERS, MAKING PHONE CALLS. THE DAY IS ALMOST OVER. AT 1:00 P.M. TSUKIJI IS EMPTY.

INTRODUCTION

THE INGREDIENTS

THE FISH MARKET

THE SUSHI

THE RECIPES

VOYAGE TO THE LAND OF SUSHI

TIPS

The ocean is a wide and secret world peopled with strange and wonderful creatures—millions of species of fish and seafood: fat fish, flat fish, voracious predators, shy creatures that hide in the sand; small crabs, tight shells, scary beasts with curling tentacles. Although today sushi is made with almost every ingredient under the sun, here you will find the authentic Japanese sushi, made by some of the best sushiya of Japan. Most of them come from the sea and we introduce them to you in Japanese as they are called by the sushiya, as well as in English. Some have several English names: American, English, Australian, regional. Some have none. As is often the case with food, local names vary widely and the Latin scientific label is the only reliable name common to all regions of the world. A sushiya should always have about twenty choices on the menu, depending on the season and group. These groups are specific to the world of sushi and can be difficult to comprehend by the outsider, which is why we have divided this chapter into nine groups of *sushi-dane* (sushi ingredients), which don't always conform to the sushiya's groups (e.g. salmon doesn't belong to any group, but we have included it in with red fish because of its color). "Best season" designates the best time of the year to eat each sushi in Japan, since we couldn't give you the best season for all the regions of the world, and after all, sushi is Japanese. "Best season" is a loose translation of a very Japanese concept, the *shun*. In a country where traditional houses made of wood and paper can be reduced to ashes in a few seconds, "impermanence" haunts the Japanese mind. All things pass in this floating world—thus, the passing moment is infinitely precious. Haiku sing the instant when the cherry blossom falls and the first drop of melting snow in spring. And in cuisine, *shun* translates this respect for the ephemeral—the fleeting moment when a food is at its best, depending on the season and place of origin.

red fish

MAGURO
NORTHERN BLUEFIN TUNA

Scientific name:	*Thunnus thynnus*
Best season:	November to February
Beverage:	Tsukasabotan (junmai karakuchi); Puligny-Montrachet (white, France); Savigny-les-Beaune (red, France)

FISH COME AND GO AT THE SUSHI COUNTER, FOLLOWING THE SHORT-LIVED CYCLE OF THE SEASONS... WHAT TO DRINK WITH EACH SUSHI? THERE IS NO SINGLE BEVERAGE THAT MATCHES WELL TO ALL *SUSHI-DANE*, SO WE HAVE CHOSEN A SAKE AND A WINE FOR EACH. SAKE ARE DEFINED BY THEIR BRAND AND THEIR NAME, THE LATTER IS INDICATED IN PARENTHESES. THEIR ENGLISH MEANINGS, WHERE POSSIBLE, ARE INDICATED IN ITALICS.

A great traveler of the oceans, Japanese tuna lays its eggs in the coastal waters of Taiwan, then swims up the 2,175 miles of the Japanese archipelago to the northern tip of Hokkaido, gobbling up mackerel, sardines, shrimp, bonitos, and squid that it finds on its way. It can measure up to 13 feet long and weigh 1,985 lb.

Maguro is somewhat close to red meat, with a taste of blood, but has a softer texture, supple and melting, and a slight acidic flavor.

High-quality tuna is killed as soon as it is caught, on the boat, and drained of its blood. Rich in iron, its meat blackens rapidly in contact with air (oxidation). Beware of sushiya serving black and dry tuna, or a dark-pink tuna: the latter is of a different species, less expensive and less tasty. The "red tuna" of sushi, the reddest meat in the tuna, also called *akami*, literally "red flesh" is different from the Red Tuna, a different species of tuna.

CHU-TORO
HALF FATTY TUNA

Scientific name:	*Thunnus thynnus*
Best season:	November to February
Beverage:	Tsukinokatsura (Katsura); Bâtard-Montrachet (white, France)

C hu-toro is the part of tuna found between the back and the belly. For a less acidic tuna than *maguro*, choose *chu-toro*. Not as well known as either *akami* or *toro*, *chu-toro*, literally middle *toro*, is the most coveted by the connoisseur. As it is the meat between the back and the belly, the proportion of fat and meat can vary and express all the nuances of the fish. If you are lucky, you will encounter a well-balanced *chu-toro*, and experience the best of both worlds in a single melting mouthful. The temperature—a determining factor—is even more important for *chu-toro* or *toro*, due to the fat. The ideal temperature for sushi rice is a little higher than that of the human body. When the sushiya presses the tuna with the rice, the thin slice is delicately warmed by the rice and the heat of the hand. The fat melts imperceptibly, forming a perfect match with the vinegared rice and wasabi: the aromas and flavors mingle. This subtle mix makes the difference between sushi and sashimi with rice.

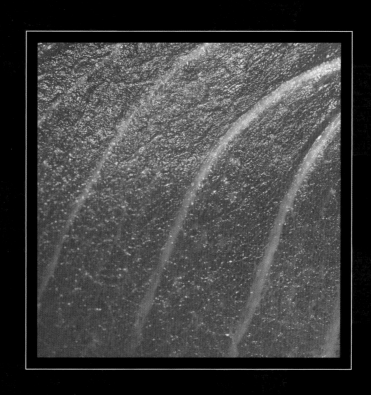

とろ

TORO
FATTY TUNA

Scientific name:	*Thunnus thynnus*
Best season:	November to February
Beverage:	Wakatake (Onikoroshi junmai) *"Young bamboo" ("Demon killer")*; Montrachet (white, France)

Toro is the fatty meat of the belly. It is one of the most popular *sushi-danes*, as it is supple, soft, and melts in the mouth. Marbled to perfection, its fat is wonderfully balanced by the vinegared rice and the wasabi; its meat is firm and pink, and if it flows in the throat, it shouldn't leave a sensation of fat, either on the tongue or on the fingers. Yet more than a quarter of its weight is fat. Where 3½ oz of red tuna is only 125 Kcal, the same quantity of *toro* may reach 344 Kcal. *Oo-toro* or great *toro* is *toro* when it is very marbled and pink: it is only a very small part of the *toro*, and of course, is more expensive. If certain fish may not be on the sushiya's menu, tuna, whether red, *chu-toro* or *toro*, is a must—without tuna, a sushi meal won't be complete.

red fish

鉄火巻

TEKKAMAKI
TUNA ROLL

Best season:	November to February
Beverage:	Umenishiki (Sake hitosuji); Fleurie (red, France)

Tekka means "fire of iron" and alludes to the bright red color of hot iron. Tekkamaki is usually made with red tuna, but you can ask for it to be made with *toro*. Whichever part of the fish is used, a tuna in a roll of rice and nori does not have the same taste as a nigiri. The dilemma of the sushi lover is not to have tuna, but to know when to eat it—after the *kohada*, the eel, before the sea urchin? Pictured above is a luxurious maki, made with all three tunas: red, half-fat, and fat. Oyakata rolls, cuts and puts six maki in front of you. He glares, hands on hips: "Eat!" his attitude is eloquent. It's impossible not to cease talking to your sushi companion and concentrate on this little marvel. An entire tuna summarized in a single roll. The nori is still crunchy. The rice is at the right temperature. You know the wasabi is hidden somewhere inside, and you haven't forgotten the drop of shoyu...

red fish

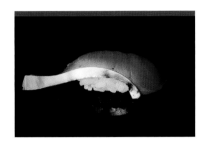

KATSUO
SKIPJACK TUNA, BONITO, OCEANIC BONITO, ATLANTIC BONITO, STRIPED BELLIED BONITO, STRIPED TUNA, STRIPY

鰹

Scientific name:	*Katsuwonus pelamis*
Best season:	April, May, and August to October
Beverage:	Tsukasabotan (Senchu Hassaku); Beaujolais (red, France); Mâcon (white, France)

Katsuo resembles the mackerel and the tuna, its faraway cousins of the Scombridae species, but its smooth skin and tapered body make it a real torpedo of temperate and tropical seas. A relative newcomer to the sushiya's menu, it has only been around the sushi counter for the last forty years. Its red meat is close in color to that of tuna, but without the complexity of flavors or the refined fat that make tuna a favorite.

Katsuo has two seasons, spring and fall. Jiro Ono, the great sushi master of Sukiyabashi Jiro, Tokyo, says: "I only serve the *katsuo* of first spring. Between spring and fall *katsuo*, there is the same difference as new tea and black tea, cherry blossom and chrysanthemum." Although *katsuo* cannot rival the great fishes of sushi, it was still loved by the inhabitants of Edo, as this old saying bears witness: "One would put one's wife in hock to eat *katsuo*!"

SAKE
CHINOOK SALMON, KING SALMON, SPRING SALMON

鮭

Scientific name:	*Oncorhynchus tschawyscha*
Best season:	September to December
Beverage:	Ichinokura (Enyu); Pouilly Fumé (white, France)

There are two main species of salmon: the Atlantic (*Salmo salar*) and the Pacific (*Oncorhynchus nerka*). Salmon can swim for hundreds of miles. A freshwater fish at birth, it lives in the ocean for up to four years and returns to its birthplace to lay its eggs. Traditionally, salmon is eaten grilled in Japan. Here are two nigiri: one with adult salmon, the other with young salmon. The adult fish is only 2 to 3 years older, but the difference, in texture more than in color, leaps to the eye. Young salmon is a rarity: practically a miracle (1 out of 40,000 fish), it is caught among adults of 15 lb. Its meat, equal to none in refinement, melts in the mouth, but it also costs five times more. Most sushiya serve farmed salmon: its fat is heavy and its smell much stronger. Some restaurants sell farmed salmon at the price of wild, but you can always tell the difference by the smell and the fat.

針
魚

SAYORI
JAPANESE HALFBEAK, JAPANESE NEEDLEFISH, HALFBEAK FISH

Scientific name:	*Hyporhamphus sajori*
Best season:	March and April
Beverage:	Sawanoi (junmai dai-karakuchi); Graves cru classé (white, France)

Sayori, literally "needle fish," is the first shiny fish of spring. It has a long, thin, almost transparent, body with a bluish shine. It is said to eat algae and have a black stomach. *Sayori* has a round firm meaty body, but very little fat. What fat there is, is surprisingly light and refined. The fish is rapidly salted, then washed in water or vinegar in order to firm the flesh. The salt needs to be washed away very quickly otherwise the meat whitens and loses its beautiful sheen. Unless the fish is perfectly fresh, the rinsing vinegar becomes cloudy. When it is clumsily cut and its insides are pierced, there is a distinctive unpleasant odor. Because it's such a pretty *sushi-dane*, sushiya tend to over-decorate it: above, a *sayori* formed in a ribbon-like shape. It really isn't necessary; a simple slice is all it takes to show off its natural beauty.

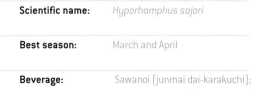

shiny fish

鱚

KISU
JAPANESE SILLAGO

Scientific name:	*Sillago japonica*
Best season:	June and July
Beverage:	Gokyo (junmai) *"Five bridges"*; Crozes-Hermitage (white, France)

An aristocratic summer *sushi-dane*, *kisu* closely follows *sayori*, in season and in quality, although its meat is more refined. This rocky fish likes clear and limpid seawater. Its fine transparent silhouette reminds you of bright and sunny summer days but *kisu* actually doesn't change much throughout the year. It is "firmed" with salt and vinegar. It can't be eaten just anytime: it shouldn't be the first in the sushi meal, and it would be a waste to eat it after fatty tuna. So where should we place these refined and subtle flavors? It should really be served only to discerning gourmets, and never ever be on the revolving belt. It does make a good fish for *tempura*, deep-fried in batter. The sushiya hides a dot of *oboro* (see page 75) under the slice of *kisu*, as a subtle seasoning that adds a discreet sweetness, volume, and highlights the deliciously bland flavors of *kisu*.

鯵

AJI
JAPANESE JACK MACKEREL, JAPANESE SCAD

Scientific name:	*Trachurus japonicus* `
Best season:	June, July, August
Beverage:	Koshigoi (junmai); Savennières (white, France)

Aji is a cheap coastal fish, fished all over Japan and the world. One day, I ate the best *aji* in my life. "Where does it come from?" I asked the sushiya. "From Awaji, off the coast of Osaka," he answered. "There are two big whirlpools over there that attract them, because all the food they love is gathered there. And so, they are well fed and fat. The fishermen catch them one by one, with a line, in small boats, even though it's quite dangerous because of the whirlpools."

Aji is a lovely fish to have during the hot season, because its aroma and taste give a oddly refreshing feeling. Its fat is light and pleasant. *Aji* used to be marinated or washed with vinegar, but now it is more often eaten raw with grated ginger and no wasabi. Fresh, it can be a true feast. Sometimes, when it is particularly good, the sushiya hides the ginger under the *aji*, so that the first thing that touches your palate is the taste of *aji*.

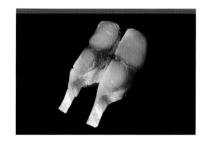

鯖

SABA
CHUB, AMERICAN, BIG-EYED, BLUE, GREENBACK
OR PACIFIC MACKEREL

Scientific name:	*Scomber japonicus*
Best season:	October and November
Beverage:	Nishinoseki (tezukuri junmaishu); Côtes-de-Provence (white, France)

The color gradation of mackerel, silvery blue, white and red, from the skin to the heart of the meat next to the backbone, is not only beautiful but reveals a symphony of flavors. *Saba* has a supple texture and a refined and tasty fat. Fall mackerel is a delicacy. There is an old Japanese saying: "Do not give any fall mackerel to the daughter-in-law." A sinister saying from a time when a daughter-in-law wasn't allowed any choice pieces. Mackerel is marinated with salt and vinegar, giving it a prick of acidity that opens up its full range of ocean flavors and aromas. But here again, the skill of the sushiya says all. The sushiya awaits, stopwatch in hand, the perfect degree of "cooking." If the meat is white all through, it's over-marinated and will be dry and hard, but if under-marinated, it will be flabby and unpleasantly fat. Contrary to its reputation, fresh mackerel does not smell. If it has a fishy smell, it's probably not fresh, or possibly even bad, and will have an unpleasant taste, even when marinated.

小
鰭

Scientific name:	*Konosirus punctatus*
Best season:	November to February
Beverage:	> with Kohada: Kaika (Kaze-no-Ichirin) *"Open flower"* (*"A flower in the wind"*); > with Shinko: Meibo (Yowa-no-Tsuki) (*"Moon of midnight"*); Soave (white, Italy)

shiny fish

KOHADA
KONOSHIRO GIZZARD SHAD, DOTTED GIZZARD SHAD, SPOTTED SARDINE

Indigenous to Japanese and Chinese seas, *kohada* is of the same Clupeidae family as the herring and the sardine. At the beginning of summer, when only about 2 inches long, it is called *shinko* or "new child." Three or four of these make one nigiri. *Shinko* has a delicate texture and subtle taste that make it a coveted sushi fish. At 4¾–5 inches, it is called *kohada*. These *sushi-dane* are short-lived luxuries. At 6¼ inches or longer, it becomes a *nakatsumi*, then a *konoshiro*, but these are not served in good sushiya. *Kohada* is the least expensive of *sushi-dane*, and is good only in sushi. It is "cooked" with salt and vinegar. The sushiya first acts on the "time of salt" and "time of vinegar," taking into account the ambient temperature. The salt penetrates the flesh and underlines its sweetness. The sushiya then washes the *kohada* with vinegar, and lets it stand in fresh vinegar to firm the flesh and change the texture of the fat. Of all the shiny fish, it has the strongest "fishy" taste. Once it has been soaked in vinegar, it is taken out to rest for one night before being served.

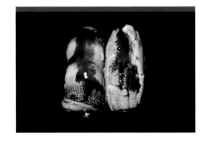

穴
子

Scientific name:	*Astroconger myriaster*
Best season:	April to June
Beverage:	Narutotai (junmai ginjyo genshu); Meursault (white, France); Saumur-Champigny (red, France)

ANAGO
NO ENGLISH NAME, SOMETIMES CALLED WHITESPOTTED CONGER OR SEA EEL

In Japanese, there are two ways to write *anago*: "child of the hole" or "eel of the sea". During the day, the *anago* stays hidden in the nooks and holes in the sand; at night, it comes out to feed. Although very close to eel, *anago* has a finer textured flesh, softer, and a lighter fat. Most sushiya outside of Japan serve eel, since *anago* is caught only in Japan, Korea and the East China Sea. *Anago* is a cooked *sushi-dane* and has its own sauce, the *tsume*, a cooking liquid simmered to thicken with sugar, mirin, and shoyu. In the blink of an eye, the sushiya places a piece of *anago* on the rice with some wasabi, presses the nigiri, gives a quick dab of *tsume* with a brush, and puts the sushi in front of you. As you bring the sushi to your mouth, its sweet and sour aroma tickles your nostrils. You put the sushi in your mouth, still warm. The taste of rice on the tongue, the taste of anago on the palate ... you close your mouth and it all melts. Later, a pleasant taste of sweet fat lingers in your mouth.

鯛

TAI
RED SEA BREAM, JAPANESE SEA BREAM, SILVER SEA BREAM, RED PORGY

Scientific name:	*Pagrus major*
Best season:	February to April
Beverage:	Shutendoji (Yamahai junmai) *"Boy drinker of sake"*; Montrachet (white, France)

Tai has been eaten in Japan for more than 5,000 years. Its noble exterior and its red skin, the color of the celebration of life, make it the king of fish. Today, it is still served on special occasions. Its Japanese name, *tai*, appears in many idioms and sayings: *medetai* "a happy or auspicious event"; to "catch a *tai* in a net of sardines" is a windfall, and to "fish a *tai* with shrimp," means to make a profit with little capital. *Tai* has a light, sweet and very clear aroma, a refined delicately pink flesh, neither too soft nor too crunchy, with a pleasant taste. The whole fish is eaten in Japanese cuisine. The meat under the skin and the skin itself are tasty, and the head is regarded as a delicacy. The sushiya scales it carefully, fillets and skins it, and dips the skin in boiling water, to soften it. Unfortunately, 80 percent of *tai* are farmed and have twice as much fat as its wild counterpart. Some sushiya outside of Japan serve Gilthead sea bream, of the Sparidae family.

鰈

KAREI
MARBLED FLOUNDER

Scientific name:	*Pleuronectes yokohamae*
Best season:	September to December
Beverage:	Suwaizumi (Mantensei) *("Sky full of stars")*; Chablis premier cru (white, France)

Its back is spotted, the same color as the seabed, where it hides. It lives at the bottom of the ocean, its belly against the sand. Its head is small, with eyes on the right. Its belly is white. Its meat, thicker in the back, is best on the belly where there is less of it. It is milk-white, of a fine texture, and marked with lines that look like the rings in wood. A white fish like sea bass, *karei* has a delicate aroma and a more subtle taste. A flat fish like *hirame*, it is relatively dry at the beginning of summer: then its flesh thickens and becomes rich. During the season, its body is thick and round with just the right amount of fat. Cut in very thin translucent slices, it has a melting, almost sweet taste. *Karei* belongs to the Pleuronectidae family, just like European plaice or dab, which may be used by sushiya outside Japan as a substitute for *karei*.

white fish

繧
鯵

Scientific name:	*Pseudocaranx dentex*
Best season:	June to August
Beverage:	Hokuyo (junmai Ecchokaiko); Jasnières (white, France)

SHIMA-AJI
WHITE TREVALLY, SILVER TREVALLY, RANGER, GUELLY JACK

Shima means "stripe" and *aji*, "jack mackerel." A cousin of the jack mackerel, *shima-aji* is a beautiful fish with a tropical look: a bright yellow middle line separates its blue green back from a pure white belly; a small black dot, like an earring, marks the edge of the gills. In Japan, it is caught in coastal areas near Tokyo. Its meat is a pretty pale pink; its taste is supple, fatty, delicate and pleasant. But this fish is mainly appreciated for its firm crunchy but tender texture. Like many fish, it is killed and bled immediately after being caught. Although its flesh must be crisp, its flavors also need a little time to ripen: it is eaten almost, but not quite, stiff. This is why the timing of eating is tricky. Today 90 percent of *shima-aji* eaten in Japan is farmed. But the farming of this fish has been more successful than that of sea perch or salmon. Japan is the only country to farm *shima-aji*.

鱸

Scientific name:	*Lateolabrax japonicus*
Best season:	June to August
Beverage:	Ichinokura (Shorai); Oregon Chardonnay (white, USA)

SUZUKI
JAPANESE SEA PERCH, JAPANESE SEA BASS

Suzuki is a manly looking fish with the head of a predator. Its flesh is perfectly white, with strong visible fiber. Its texture is firm, its fat light, and its aroma distinctive. As with all white fish, it is cut in thin slices of no more than an eighth of an inch thickness for sushi. Thicker, it would be too crunchy and practically inedible. *Suzuki* is not only eaten raw, but also in *arai*, which means "washed": thin slices of *suzuki* are dipped in ice cold water and ice. The fish is "cooked" not by heat, but by extreme cold. The meat whitens, "curls" a little, and the texture becomes even firmer. This technique, which highlights the crisp texture of this fish, is possible only with the very best fish. Japanese sea bass is different from European sea bass (*Dicentrarchus labrax*), commonly called sea bass, bass or sea perch in Europe. Since it is an expensive fish, it is sometimes farmed and can be very bad: beware of fat bass, it probably needs exercise!

HIRAME
BASTARD HALIBUT, FALSE FLOUNDER, OLIVE FLOUNDER

鮃

Scientific name:	*Paralichythys olivaceus*
Best season:	December to February
Beverage:	Ohyama (tokubetsu junmaishu) *"Big mountain"*; Riesling grand cru (white, France)

Very good *hirame* has an exquisite and almost undetectable flavor; its flesh is soft, fine and delicate. Among the white fish, *kan- hirame*, the winter *hirame* of February, is the best. *Hirame* is killed and bled (*ikejime* technique) immediately after it is caught, to render the flesh perfectly translucent. The light green of wasabi under the pure white slice of fish is faintly visible: the sushi is wearing the first colors of spring, young green and melting snow. A slice weighs less than half an ounce and is never more than a quarter inch thick. The sushiya, always respectful of balance and harmony, makes a nigiri of *hirame* with less rice than for a *toro*. Sushi connoisseurs love the meat of the fins: firmed by constant exercise, it has the right amount of fat and is deliciously crunchy. Some sushiya outside Japan use turbot or brill, similar in shape but with a much coarser taste. Beware: certain restaurants sell farmed flounder (turbot) at the price of wild.

white fish

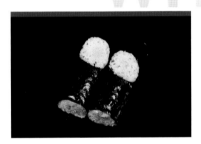

OBORO-MAKI
WHITE FISH OR SHRIMP PASTE ROLL

おぼろ巻

Best season:	all year round
Beverage:	green tea; Aramasa (Akita-ryu junmaishu) (*"Akita-style"*); Saint-Véran (white, France)

Oboro is cooked white fish or shrimp, mashed into a dry paste, and is very sweet. Fish *oboro* is always made with white fish because its sweet soft taste is impossible to achieve with shiny fish. To prepare an *oboro* of shrimp, the sushiya peels and purees small shrimp. He adds salt, sugar, sake, a drop of shoyu and cooks it in a double boiler, stirring constantly. *Oboro* has an almost feathery feel, a white or pale pink color that reflects its soft taste, melting like snow on the tongue. An *oboro-maki* is deliciously mild, and especially with good nori, it makes a perfect match with green tea—like a "teacake." After all, black, white and pink are the colors of Japanese sweets! In certain high-class sushiya, *oboro* is used with wasabi to season summer shiny fish, such as *kisu* and *sayori*: a dash of sweetness under the slice of fish.

蝦

EBI
JAPANESE KURUMA SHRIMP

Scientific name:	*Marsupenaeus japonicus*
Best season:	May to July
Beverage:	Wakaebisu (junmai ginjyo Gizaemon); Pouilly-Fuissé (white, France)

crustaceans

Usually when the sushiya puts a sushi in front of you, your first reflex is to eat it. But when this sushi is put on your black lacquered plate, all you can do is admire it. Luminous red, pure white; brilliance, harmony, flamboyance, the shrimp is a perfect beauty. Such beauty is only achieved with very fresh shrimp: it comes to the sushiya, flipping its tail and very much alive. After boiling in lots of water, the chef peels it to order. He leaves the liver, an almost invisible brown needlepoint of the deepest richness. The meat of the shrimp, juicy, firm, almost elastic, is also naturally very sweet. The liver is tiny, but plays an important part: like a thick sauce or pungent spice, it seasons the shrimp and gives it a strong mature complexity. Unfortunately, most sushiya use frozen shrimp, which for obvious reasons are served without the liver.

ぼたん蝦

BOTAN-EBI
PEONY SHRIMP

Scientific name:	*Pandalus nipponensis*
Best season:	April, May (Pacific) and Sept. to November (Sea of Japan)
Beverage:	Fukunotomo (Kame-no-o-de-tsu-kutta junmai ginyoshu) *"Friend of happiness" ("Made with a turtle's tail")*; Meursault (white, France)

Shrimp may be eaten cooked or raw. If the *kuruma-ebi* opens its full range of taste and flavor when it is cooked, *botan-ebi* and *ama-ebi* (*Pandalus borealis eous*, North Sea Shrimp) contain a lot of water and harden when cooked; they are best eaten raw. These two shrimp come from Northern Japan. *Botan-ebi* is found mainly in Hokkaido. Firm and with a pleasant smell of shrimp, it is considered a high-class *sushi-dane*. If it is extremely fresh, the sushiya will even serve its eggs on a *gunkan-maki* (see pages 130–131). *Ama-ebi* has become very common, even in sushiya outside Japan. *Amai* means "sweet" in Japanese: these shrimp are sweet mellow and creamy. Although less beautiful than the *botan-ebi*, with less taste and flavor, they are much cheaper. If you like the feeling of creamy shrimp melting in the mouth, you will enjoy both *botan-ebi* and *ama-ebi*.

蝦蛄

SHAKO
MANTIS SHRIMP

Scientific name:	*Oratosquilla oratoria*
Best season:	End of April to June and October to March
Beverage:	Kamikokoro (tokubetsu junmai) *"Pure and beautiful heart"*; Cassis (white, France)

crustaceans

There are two ways and two seasons to eat *shako*. If you like it full of eggs, then you appreciate the end of spring when its belly is packed with tight rows of fox-colored eggs. If you like it without eggs, then eat it in winter, when it tastes like a hybrid of shrimp and crab. Despite its name in English, *shako* is not a shrimp, neither is it an insect, although one wonders... When cooked, it doesn't turn pink or red like the other crustaceans, but rather a light purple. This creature wasn't very much liked until the day someone had the bright idea to make sushi with it. It is boiled whole, then peeled and cut. The water must be really boiling otherwise it will become spongy and limp. Most of the time, the sushiya buys it already cooked: his personal touch will be the *tsume*, the sauce that makes up for the lack of natural taste, since *shako* has neither the sweetness of shrimp or crab, the iodine of shellfish, nor the lightness and fat of fish. You can also eat it without sauce, with just a touch of wasabi.

蟹

KANI
CRAB

Best season:	March
Beverage:	> with Kegani: Chiyokotobuki (Otora) *("Great tiger")*; Riesling (white, France) > with Zuwaigani: Harushika (Fuinshu) *"Deer of spring"*; Rioja (white, Spain) > with Tarabagani: Gozenshu (Mukashizukuri) *("Old fashioned")*; Chassagne-Montrachet (white, France)

These three crabs are a trio of flavors from Hokkaido, surrounded by three seas and with some of the best produce of the Japanese archipelago. *Kegani* (*Erimacrus isenbeckii*) or Horsehair Crab (left), is the most popular of the three, especially for its "miso," a creamy brown meat packed inside the body. It has little meat in the legs and claws, but around March its body is very full. The thickest part of the claw is made into a nigiri, with a dot of soybean paste and a thin belt of nori. The crab is cooked whole; the miso is sweet, creamy, rich and tasty. It is only available after the snow has melted in March. *Zuwaigani* (*Chionoecetes opilio*), or Snow Crab (center) has nothing in the body, but its claw meat is delicious. However. it's not very popular among the local people of Hokkaido. *Tarabagani* (*Paralithodes camtschatica*) or King Crab (right) lives in deep waters and has ten long legs, although you can't really see the smallest as they are not used anymore. The meat of the claws near the body is delicious.

TORIGAI
COCKLE, LARGE COCKLE, EGG COCKLE

鳥貝

Scientific name:	*Fulvia mutica*
Best season:	April and May
Beverage:	Urakasumi (junmai Kippon); Saint-Joseph (white, France)

Torigai is a bivalve shellfish with a shell that resembles that of the *akagai*. The surface of its meat shows complicated patterns, black and white, and a luster reminiscent of velvet. Unfortunately the season for wild *torigai* is becoming shorter and shorter: the best *torigai*, big, fat and juicy, tender in the mouth, is caught from April to May. An interesting point—all shellfish, except *torigai* and abalone, are winter sushi foods.

The sushiya opens the shell and cuts the meat in two before cleaning. He then dips it in boiling water with a drop of vinegar: this fixes the color. As soon as the color has changed, he drops it in iced water to cool it. This technique, which uses the shock of hot and cold, is common in Japanese cooking, where cooking times are usually short. While most *sushi-dane* are eaten raw, this cooking method gives *torigai* its luster, while preserving its taste.

shellfish

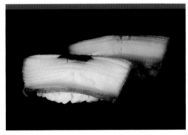

鮑

AWABI
ABALONE

Scientific name:	*Nordotis discus discus*
Best season:	July and August
Beverage:	Harushika (Daigomi); *"Deer of spring" ("The gracious teachings of Buddha")* Chevalier-Montrachet (white, France)

In midsummer, abalone can weigh more than 2 lb, but it is at its best at about $1^{3}/_{4}$–2 lb. It is said that during the winter an abalone is so thin that you are buying an empty shell. Abalones from Chiba have an excellent reputation, but abalone fishing has reduced the numbers to such an extent, that it was prohibited for five years. The male is best eaten raw while the meat of the female is more tender and is better cooked. Start with raw sashimi of abalone (the meat is too hard to go well with sushi rice): the taste of the sea spreads in your mouth. Then try a nigiri of abalone steamed in sake. Abalone is the only sushi food cooked in sake. The steam of the sake makes the abalone swell and become miraculously tender, barely elastic, with a sweet, refined and light flavor. The only drawback is its price: among the *sushi-dane*, abalone is the second most expensive after tuna, and may be as much as 7,000 yen per pound with the shell.

帆立貝

HOTATEGAI
SCALLOP

Scientific name:	*Patinopecten yessoensis*
Best season:	October to December
Beverage:	Otokoyama (Kimoto junmai) *"Mountain of men"*; Chassagne-Montrachet (white, France)

shellfish

A northern shellfish, Japanese scallop is almost always farmed. High-class sushiya, who once only used wild shellfish, don't serve them anymore. It's easy to tell the difference: wild scallops which live at the bottom of the sea have one flat shell and one rounded shell, on which other small shellfish are sometimes stuck. The farmed scallop is grown hung on a plastic cord, so both shell halves are rounded. It is often called Kai-bashira, or "Pillar of the shell." This is because its adductor muscle, the white thick round meat of the scallop, looks like a pillar supporting the upper shell. Of a milky whiteness, scallop makes a pretty compact and round nigiri. It is juicy, supple and sweet, with practically no iodine. These characteristics make it an easy shellfish for beginners. Scallops belong to the Pectinidae family, which encompasses more than 300 species—the best known in Europe and the United States are the *Pecten maximus* (Atlantic Ocean) and the *Pecten jacobeu*s (Mediterranean).

KOBASHIRA
CHINESE MACTRA, ROUND CLAM, HEN CLAM

Scientific name:	*Mactra chinensis*
Best season:	December to February
Beverage:	Tamanohikari (junmai ginjyo cho-tokusen Bizenomachi); Saint-Aubin (white, France)

T his beautiful coral-colored little jewel of the sea is even prettier dressed in the black of nori. It is a small shellfish—one *gunkan-maki* usually holds several. Slightly crunchy but tender, it is naturally sweet with a faint taste of iodine. But its flavors weaken and fade away with the end of winter: you must taste it before March. Its real Japanese name is *baka-gai*, which means "stupid shellfish," but, because it looks like a scallop, only much smaller, it is better known under the name *kobashira*, or "little pillar". It is also called *aoyagi*. Most restaurants outside Japan use small scallops or yellow clams, both of these shellfish being close to *kobashira* in shape and form but lacking its sweetness. However, their texture allows them to be used as a replacement.

海松貝

MIRUGAI
KEEN'S GAPER

Scientific name:	*Tresus keenae*
Best season:	December to March
Beverage:	Harushika (cho-karakuchi) *"Deer of spring" ("Extra dry")*; Chablis grand cru (white, France)

Mirugai is a big winter shellfish, of which only the siphon (the muscle with which it exhales water) is eaten. The siphon is rapidly boiled and gives about eight nigiri! This bivalve, despite appearances, is of the same family as the Chinese Mactra (*kobashira*), and is often called the "king of shellfish," because it is the crunchiest, the sweetest, the tastiest and the most elastic of them all.

It is within the shellfish group that you will find the richest variety of *sushi-dane*. But if you try one *akagai*, one *mirugai* and one abalone, you will have made a grand tour of all the aromas and flavors available throughout the year.

shellfish

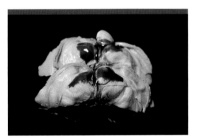

蛤

HAMAGURI
HARD CLAM

Scientific name:	*Meretrix lusoria*
Best season:	December to March
Beverage:	Hachitsuru (Kura-monogatari) *"Eight cranes" ("Stories of the sake cellar")*; Pouilly-Fuissé (white, France)

The best *hamaguri* once came from the Bay of Tokyo, but 90 percent are now imported from China. But these, being too elastic, are released in the sea at Kuwana, in the Sea of Japan where, in six months, they soften and become tastier. The ideal *hamaguri* weighs 2¾–3½ oz. First the sushiya shells and skewers them on a thin bamboo stick. Then, after rinsing under the tap, he boils them in lightly seasoned water, watching carefully as, if overcooked, they become hard, and if undercooked, they won't keep and may even poison the customers! He lets the cooking water cool and puts the *hamaguri* to rest in it overnight. He also makes the *tsume*, an almost caramelized reduction of the cooking water, strongly seasoned this time with sake, sugar, shoyu, and mirin (see anago p. 45). When serving the sushi, the sushiya dabs some tsume on the hamaguri with a brush. During the season, *hamaguri* is thick and juicy, has a wonderful smell and flavor, enhanced by a dash of wasabi.

北寄貝

HOKKIGAI
SURF CLAM, NORTHERN SHELL

Scientific name:	*Pseudocardium sachalinensis*
Best season:	December to March
Beverage:	Ohyama (tokubetsu junmai cho-karakuchi) *"Big mountain" ("Extra dry")*; Graves (white, France)

Hokkigai is a very sturdy bivalve: one *hokki* will make four nigiri. Cased in a black rounded shell, it is caught all year long in the north of Japan, but it is best eaten at the beginning of winter. Dipped in boiling water, it turns into a beautiful purple. It is eaten plain or lightly grilled with a drop of *sudachi*, a Japanese lime which is less sour than lemon, with a skin that hides surprising aromas. *Hokki* is crunchy without being hard, and in the mouth, reveals a mellow taste typical of shellfish, with less natural sweetness than *mirugai*, more iodine, but very refreshing nonetheless.

Surrounded by three seas—the ice-cold Sea of Okhotsk, the Sea of Japan and the Pacific Ocean—and separated from the main island of Honshu by the deep straits of Tsugaru, Hokkaido is a big island with active volcanoes, where temperatures may dip as low as minus 22ºF in the winter. Hokkigai is a speciality of this country of fire and ice.

shellfish

螺貝

TSUBUGAI
NEPTUNE, WHELK

Scientific name:	*Babylonia japonica*
Best season:	October to March
Beverage:	Kumamoto Bishonen (ginzukuri junmaishu) *"Beautiful young man of Kumamoto" ("Silver-made")*; Napa Sauvignon (white, USA)

Tsubugai is a big snail. Its body, unrolled, may be more than 7¾ inches long and weigh 1½ lb. This snail of the seas of Hokkaido is eaten raw. Very hard, it has a strong flavor of iodine. The sushiya breaks the shell and kneads the body with salt to get rid of its stickiness. He cuts it in two, lengthwise, and extracts a thick filament of white fat, which, without being actually dangerous, may cause a feeling of "drunkenness" if eaten accidentally. The two halves of the body are cut into several slices, again, lengthwise. These roll back into half spirals, and are just the size of one nigiri. One *tsubugai* gives five or six nigiri. Cheap, it is popular with young people who still have all their teeth! It definitely needs to be firmly chewed. Since it is probably not worth sending all the way to Tokyo, this sushi-dane can only be tasted in Hokkaido.

赤貝

AKAGAI
ARK SHELL, BLOOD CLAM

Scientific name:	*Scapharca broughtonii*
Best season:	January to March
Beverage:	Hiraizumi (yamahai junmaishu) *"Flat spring of water"*; Chablis (white, France)

shellfish

The only red-blooded shellfish, the *akagai*'s color makes it one of the stars of the sushi counter. The best come from Yuriage, in the district of Miyagi. *Akagai* fishing is prohibited during the two summer months to allow reproduction. In any event, it's not the right season for sushi: its eggs have used up all its energy and its meat is soft and flabby.

During the season, the meat is thick, crunchy but smooth. It has a beautiful coral color that is enhanced by a few light slashes with the knife given just before it is served (the actual purpose of this is to make it easier to eat). Ask the sushiya for a *himo-kyu*, a maki made with the frilly gills of *akagai* and cucumber. A refreshing, crunchy sushi, a summer delicacy—true sushi lovers could kill for this maki at the height of the season.

Some sushiya outside Japan use other red shellfish as a replacement. The color may be close, but the taste and the texture are not.

海栗

UNI
SEA URCHIN

Scientific name:	*Anthocidaris crassispina*
Best season:	March to August
Beverage:	Urakasumi (junmai ginjyo Zen); Vouvray sec (dry, white, France)

Uni, like *anago* and *kohada*, is not a *sushi-dane* with which you would start your sushi meal. Its position is of strategic importance, since it is rich, creamy, sweet with lots of iodine and little soft grains in the meat which melt immediately in the mouth. It is sometimes written "sea chestnut" in Japanese. Two varieties are served in Japan: the one known as "white," because of the light color of its meat, is very sweet and creamy. The other, "red," is darker, but also richer and tastier. Hokkaido, Sanriku, Shimonoseki and Nagasaki—Japanese sea urchins come from all over Japan. In certain areas, fishing is restricted to avoid the extinction of the species. Today, sea urchins are often imported from the United States, Canada, and Korea. European sea urchins are different: their meat is thinner with much more iodine. Some sushi lovers prefer it to Japanese sea urchin for the stronger taste of the sea.

い く ら

IKURA
SALMON ROE

Best season:	September and October
Beverage:	Kamoizumi (Yamabuki-iro-no-sake) *("Sake of Golden Yellow")*; Saint-Péray (sparkling, white, France)

Small crystal balls of a deep orange color, perfectly smooth, they roll on the tongue and burst between your teeth, freeing a salty juice tasting of the sea with an aftertaste of hen's egg yolk. Raw salmon roe come from the north. Some sushiya prepare them, some will buy them already prepared, and add a little seasoning to flavor and soften the aftertaste that can sometimes be quite strong.

The roe is carefully separated by hand in salted water at 140°F, then immediately rinsed in fresh water to cool rapidly. Then they are seasoned with shoyu, sake, and mirin. More of a seasoning than a marinade, they are not soaked for too long or they lose their beautiful limpid roundness. Each egg must be perfectly round and smooth: too much salt in the water in which they are prepared will extract their natural juices, leaving them wrinkled or soggy.

fish roe

数 の 子

KAZUNOKO
PACIFIC HERRING ROE

Scientific name:	*Clupea pallasi*
Best season:	March and April
Beverage:	Hiraizumi (yamahai junmaishu); Champagne Brut Nature (still champagne, France)

Kazu means "number" and *ko* means "child"—and there are many children in there! How many eggs do we eat when swallowing a nigiri of *kazunoko*? Hard to say, the eggs are as tightly packed as they were in their mother's belly. Two roes for a herring: wrapped in a thin skin, each roe is eaten whole, plain, and each tiny egg bursts under the tooth, with a small explosive sound... which reminds one of champagne! *Kazunoko* is salted: the sushiya soaks it for one night in fresh water. It is pictured here accompanied with a leaf of *shiso*, a refreshing, tangy, flavorful leaf, and a belt of nori. It is served with grated *katsuobushi*: steamed, dried and grated bonito, used as a condiment to add a smoky flavor, or to make the soup base for many Japanese dishes. Originally from Hokkaido, this *sushi-dane* was unknown in Tokyo until recent times. Today, you will find it in many sushiya, in Japan and elsewhere, herring being a common fish around the world.

蝦の卵

BOTAN-EBI NO TAMAGO
PEONY SHRIMP ROE

Best season:	May and June
Beverage:	Yonetsuru (Sanae) *"Rice crane"*; Crémant d'Alsace (white, France)

The sea has created an artist's palette of astonishing colors. The Imperial shrimp is brown and white, with a translucent body: cooked, it turns bright red and white. Small and ugly, the Shiba shrimp is light brown, but takes on a charming pink color when cooked. Peony shrimp, red and white, has such a fine carapace you can see through to its body. Sometimes you will see a deep blue color lightly tinged with green: raw, the eggs make an excellent nigiri. It's a specialty of Sapporo, the capital of Hokkaido. Peony shrimp roe does not have the fat of caviar or salmon roe, but a fresh aroma enhanced by horseradish. The sushiya uses horseradish, which is called *Ainu wasabi* in Hokkaido, instead of wasabi.

fish roe

白子

SHIRAKO
PACIFIC COD MILT

Scientific name:	*Gadus marcocephalus*
Best season:	December and January
Beverage:	Dewanoyuki (shizenshu) *"Snow of opening wings"* (*"Natural sake"*); Jurançon (white, France)

Shirako is the milt or the sperm of Pacific cod and is a *sushi-dane* of the north. It is pictured here decorated with grated white radish and red pepper, its milky whiteness standing out against the black of nori. Its sticky glue-like texture comes as a surprise in the mouth, and spreads like a very mature cheese, but with a strong taste of the sea.

Cod is as common in Japan as in other parts of the world. In Japan, it is a winter fish that is often eaten in *nabe*, a pot cooked at the table, with pieces of fish, vegetables, tofu, and sometimes noodles. Steam rises, condensing on the windows of the dining room and warms everybody up: a typical Japanese winter family scene. As for the milt, the best season is obviously when the female lays her eggs, from December to January.

IKA
SQUID, CUTTLEFISH

A denizen of the sea that is neither fish nor shellfish, *ika* comes in thousands of species. Different species are used in sushi, depending on the season, but whatever the season, squid is a necessity. "At the sushiya, there must be red tuna, white fish and shiny fish, and *ika*, which is neither one nor the other," writes the great sushiya, Yukio Morooka. The meat of the winter *sumi-ika* or Common cuttlefish, is pleasantly thick, twice as thick as that of the summer *aori-ika*, tender and slightly elastic. Your teeth sink in with delight and discover a deep sweetness. *Aori-ika* (*Sepioteuthis lessoniana*) should be eaten during July and August. It is the sweetest of *sushi-dane*, after shrimp, with soft meat, slightly sticky and naturally sweet. The body is eaten raw and the tentacles, if eaten, are cooked. A little wasabi and a few dabs of fresh grated ginger enhance this precious marine gift of summer.

Scientific name:	*Sepia esculenta*
Best season:	November to February
Beverage:	> with Sumi-ika: Shirataki (junmai Uonuma) *"White waterfall"*; Tokay grand cru (white, France); > with Aori-ika: Hiokizakura (junmaishu) *"Cherry blossom of one day"*; Gavi del Commune del Gavi (white, Italy)

squid & octo-pus

TAKO
OCTOPUS

C ooked octopus has the slightly smoky aroma of nuts and an elastic but tender texture. The sushiya cooks the tentacle whole, which becomes purplish brown. He watches for the moment when the center of the meat is no longer translucent and removes it immediately from the boiling water—overcooked octopus is dry and hard. The thicker the tentacles, the better the octopus. Don't miss the octopus that the sushiya has just cooked as it cools in its basket: ask him to cut it and eat it plain, without *shoyu*, with just a little freshly grated wasabi. The bright green stands out on the white meat as if in snow. Let the aftertaste develop. Then, have a sushi. The sushiya makes small cuts in the meat to make it easier to eat. A dab of sweet *tsume* with the brush enhances the discreet taste of octopus. Avoid octopus during the fall: the female guards her eggs during a month without feeding or moving. She loses 90 percent of her body weight and dies when the eggs are hatched.

Scientific name:	*Octopus vulgaris Cuvier*
Best season:	January and February
Beverage:	Kotsuzumi (Cha Tanba Touji) *"Small hand drum"* (*"Sake maker of Chatanba"*); Beaune (white, France)

hen's eggs

玉子焼

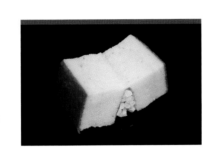

TAMAGOYAKI
SWEET OMELET

Best season:	all year round
Beverage:	Umenishiki (Sake Hitosuji); Gewurtztraminer, late harvest (white, France)

Connoisseurs judge the skill of a sushiya by his *tamagoyaki*. Some sushiya buy their *tamagoyaki* ready-made at Tsukiji market, while others will spend an hour a day making it. This is how Jiro of Yokohama makes his: he purees Shiba shrimp and adds grated yam, eggs, sugar, salt and sake. It takes more than an hour of constant work to mix all these ingredients thoroughly and cook a ¾-inch thick *tamago*. Brown on the surface, golden yellow inside, sweet, moist, slightly spongy and supple, *tamago* perfectly matches the rice seasoned with vinegar. The shrimp puree adds a rich complex taste to the egg which, by itself, would be too bland to complement an evening of fish, crustaceans and shellfish. Yam is used for the same purpose as egg whites in Western desserts—it makes the *tamago* lighter.

The Shiba shrimp is less than 4 inches long. Its carapace is thin and its meat very tender. It is caught in the Bay of Tokyo since the Edo era, and the Bay of Ise and the Setonaikai. It is also imported from Korea.

海苔巻

makis

NORIMAKI
NORI ROLL

Best season:	all year round
Beverage:	Mado-no-Ume (Hanasaika) *"Plum blossom at the window" ("Open flower")*; Gewurtztraminer (white, France or Germany)

Norimaki in Tokyo, *maki-zushi* in Kansai (Western Japan) and commonly, although mistakenly, *futomaki*, looks like a big birthday present. It contains many good things: Shiitake mushrooms cooked in shoyu, sugar and mirin; snow pea pods, Chinese peas or sugar peas, cooked plain, very green and crunchy; *tamagoyaki*; *oboro*; and *natane-tamago*, another preparation of egg resembling scrambled eggs. A single common aspect to these ingredients is their sweet taste. You can see all of them—don't forget the sushi rice and the nori that unite them—in these colorful rolls.

The sushiya rolls this voluminous sushi carefully and firmly so that everything stays put, but without squashing the rice or breaking the nori. He must do so very quickly so that the nori doesn't absorb any moisture and get wrinkled and soggy.

河童巻

KAPPA-MAKI
CUCUMBER MAKI

Best season:	all year round
Beverage:	Masumi (Okuden kanzukuri); Seyssel (white, France)

When you take a maki between your fingers the very fine velvet of nori, just faintly moist, lets you guess the texture of the rice underneath, a portent of good things to come. You can eat *nigiri-zushi* with your fingers or with chopsticks, but *hoso-maki* or thin roll, must be eaten with your fingers. This *kappa-maki* contains a very thin whole cucumber. Slightly thicker than a little finger, this cucumber has a wonderful fresh "green" aroma, as well as a clean, crisp crunch. *Kappa* is a salamander, a malicious animal of Japanese mythology, which plays mischievous tricks on humans.

新香巻

SHINKO-MAKI
MAKI OF WHITE RADISH

Best season:	all year round
Beverage:	Manatsuru (yamahai jikomi jun-maishu); "True crane" Muscat, late harvest (white, France)

Shinko or *takuwan* is giant white or long radish, also known as Daikon radish, dried and fermented in salt (the yellow color is added). It is sweet and salty, with strong crunchy fibers. Rice is served at every traditional Japanese meal and always comes with salted fermented vegetables (radish, Chinese cabbage, eggplant, cucumber). It's like bread and cheese in France: a cereal-based staple with a fermented salty food.

makis

干瓢巻

KANPYO-MAKI
MAKI OF KANPYO

Best season:	all year round
Beverage:	Shinanonishiki (Retoro Label) ("Retro label"); Condrieu (white, France)

Kanpyo is green gourd called *yugao* or "face of the evening," cut in long slices and dried. The preparation of *kanpyo* takes two days. First the sushiya soaks the sliced dried gourd in water, drains and kneads it with salt. Then he boils it in a large quantity of water. He drains it again and opens it, discarding the parts that are too hard, cutting the parts that are too big. Then he simmers them with sugar, shoyu and mirin. When the liquid is absorbed, he drains it to cool quickly. Very sweet and juicy, *kanpyo-maki* makes a good dessert to round off a sushi evening. It is always cut into four pieces instead of the usual six for *hoso-maki* of cucumber, *oboro* and *shinko*, so that you bite into it, letting the sweet juices flow in your mouth. *Kanpyo*, sushi rice and nori: a wonderful vegetarian sushi of well cooked juicy fiber, sweet rice vinegar and the soft taste of smoky seaweed.

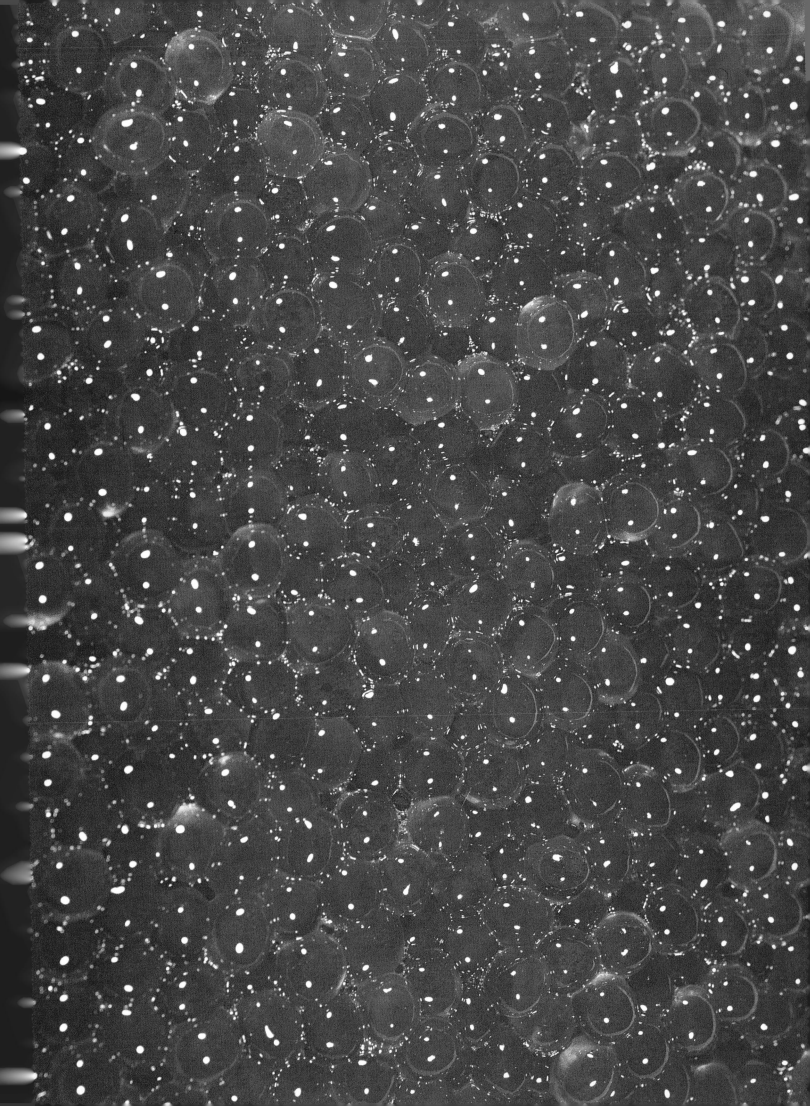

INTRODUCTION

THE INGREDIENTS

THE FISH MARKET

THE SUSHI

THE RECIPES

VOYAGE TO THE LAND OF SUSHI

TIPS

The recipes, whether traditional or original, in the following

pages all have one thing in common: vinegared rice.

This is what makes them sushi. If nigiri is the sushi of

professionals, requiring a ten-year apprenticeship, then

chirashi, maki and *ochi-sushi* or *hako-sushi* are made at

home on a regular basis. They are less widely known

internationally but very common in Japan. The practical

information you need, including the recipe for the rice

and instructions on how to cut the fish, appear at the

back of the book (see pages 182–187).

Nama hamu, sarami, chorizo no maki-mono

Parma ham, chorizo, or salami maki

MAKES 1 MAKI

5 oz vinegared rice
($^1/_2$ cup raw rice)

2 thin slices
Parma ham
or 3 very thin slices
chorizo
or 4 very thin slices
salami

8 thin green beans

makisu

1 lettuce leaf

plastic wrap

Cook the beans in boiling water, uncovered. Do not overcook—they should be crisp. Drain and dry with paper towels. **2.** Cut some pieces of plastic wrap, slightly larger than the makisu. Cover the makisu with the wrap, folding and tucking the edges under the makisu. **3.** Line up the slices of Parma ham (or chorizo or salami) on the wrap, slightly overlapping. **4.** Wet your hands, form a rough cylinder with the rice, and place it on top of the ham. Press gently with wet fingers. **5.** Line up the green beans horizontally across the rice, slightly overlapping, to make a single line of green beans. **6.** Lift the edge of the makisu nearest to you, taking care that the plastic wrap stays in place. Roll almost one complete turn, holding the beans with the tips of your fingers. Press firmly over the whole length of the makisu and complete the roll. **7.** Open the makisu without unrolling the wrap. **8.** Using a very sharp and wet knife, which you must wipe with a damp cloth after each cut, cut the roll into thick slices without removing the wrap. **9.** Discard the wrap from each slice and serve.

Furesshu samon no chirashi

Fresh salmon chirashi

**SERVES 2
(1 CHIRASHI)**

1¼ lb vinegared rice
(1½ cups raw rice)

3½ oz salmon

3½ oz salmon roe

1 egg

2 snowpeas

½ tbsp
sesame seeds

edible flowers or
parsley, to garnish
(optional)

Beat the egg and pour a small quantity into a nonstick skillet or omelet pan. Cook over medium heat, turning the pan so that the egg spreads over the base in a thin layer. Don't worry if the egg spreads out unevenly, it won't show in the chirashi. **2.** As soon as the edges of your thin omelet are dry, turn over and cook the other side. Do not brown. Set aside. **3.** Cook the snowpeas in boiling water, uncovered. Do not overcook, they should be crisp. Drain and set aside. **4.** Cut the salmon in small thin pieces. **5.** Cut the omelet in thin strips. **6.** Cut the snowpeas in thin strips. **7.** In a salad bowl, mix the salmon, omelet strips and peas with the vinegared rice. **8.** Pour into a large serving dish or salad bowl. Sprinkle over the salmon roe and sesame seeds, and garnish with edible flower petals or parsley, if using.

1¼ lb vinegared rice
(1½ cups raw rice)

3 slices tamago,
each approx. ½ oz

3 large tiger shrimp

3 scallops

3 slices mackerel,
each approx. ½ oz

3 slices flounder,
each approx. ½ oz

3 slices sea bass,
each approx. ½ oz

3 slices tuna,
each approx. ½ oz

3 slices salmon,
each approx. ½ oz

3 tbsp salmon roe

pinch of salt

pickled ginger
(see page 50)

wasabi
(optional)

soy sauce

makisu

Sushi no moriawase, san nin mae

Sushi dinner for three

The day before: 1. Make tamago (see page 104).

2. Marinate the mackerel (see recipe for bo-zushi, page 141).

The following day: 1. Skewer the shrimp on wooden skewers or wooden toothpicks to avoid curling when cooked. Boil some water with a pinch of salt. Cook the prawns. Peel and cut them lengthwise under the belly and open them out into a butterfly shape (butterfly cut). **2.** Prepare and cut the fish. Cut the white fish diagonally in thin slices; the tuna and salmon in thicker slices. With your fingers, peel off the thin skin that covers the real skin of the mackerel before cutting. **3.** Butterfly cut each scallop (cut nearly in half lengthwise but not completely; one side stays attached; spread open) so that each scallop is shaped like a figure 8.

Put together: 1. Follow the recipe for nigiri-zushi on page 186 to make nigiri. **2.** Follow the recipe for hoso-maki on pages 132–133 to make a few maki. **3.** Follow the recipe for miso soup on pages 102–103.

You will probably make a less varied platter than the one shown here. In that case, pick a slice of tuna or salmon, as these fish keep better and are easier to prepare—few or no bones, easy to cut and form into nigiri. You could also use marinated mackerel if you prefer or if you want to experiment. This often underrated fish is delicious in nigiri with some grated fresh ginger.

Sushi no moriawase, roku nin mae
Sushi party for six

5¼ lb vinegared rice
(5½ cups raw rice)

tamago

8 sheets nori

mackerel

tuna

flounder

sea bass or sea bream

salmon

sardine

large tiger shrimp

small shrimp

scallops

crab
(canned)

white tuna
(canned)

sea-urchin

octopus
(1 big tentacle)

squid

lumpfish roe

salmon roe

surimi

takuan
(pickled sweet
long white radish)

avocado

cucumber

wasabi
(optional)

pickled ginger
(optional)

soy sauce

makisu

plastic wrap

You should know that to make a sushi platter for six people, you will spend all day in the kitchen just preparing each fish, let alone the rice, the marinated mackerel and the tamago. But patience, courage, and good humor are always rewarded; your guests will definitely be impressed!

The day before: Order your fish and seafood in advance. Prepare the mackerel, tamago and other ingredients for futomaki: **1.** Follow the recipe for marinated mackerel in the recipe for bo-zushi on page 141. **2.** Follow the recipe for tamago on page 104. **3.** Follow the recipe for futomaki on pages 106–107 to prepare the ingredients.

The following day: 1. Start with the rice: follow the recipe for sumeshi, vinegared rice, on pages 184–185. **2.** Make the futomaki. Wrap it well in plastic wrap without cutting and set aside. **3.** Boil some water with two pinches of salt. With a handful of salt, knead the octopus and rinse. Cook the octopus on high heat for 15 minutes or until tender. Set aside without cutting. **4.** Peel and cut the cucumber and avocado. **5.** Open and drain the cans of crab, white tuna, salmon roe, and lumpfish roe. Mix the tuna with mayonnaise. **6.** Prepare the fish. If you fillet the fish yourself, follow the fish-cutting instructions on page 183, otherwise ask your fishman to fillet the fish, but only when you come to collect, not when you order it. Set aside the fillets in a dish. **7.** Shell the sea urchins and scallops. Set aside in a dish.

When everything is ready, make all the sushi at once:
1. Prepare a bowl of water with vinegar to wet your hands and knife as you go. **2.** First make rice balls for the nigiri, following the technique described on page 186. **3.** Cut the fish as you go—for example, if you cut four slices, make four nigiri. Cut four more slices, and make four more nigiri and so on. **4.** Once you have made all your nigiri, make the gunkan-maki, following the recipe on page 130. **5.** Finally, you can roll the maki with the ugly bits and pieces of fish that won't show in the maki. **6.** Wet your knife after each cut to cut all the maki. **7.** Line up the sushi on a big platter or serving dish. **8.** Serve accompanied by pickled ginger and soy sauce.

When you cut the fish and the octopus, hold your knife at an angle of 45° or less to the cutting board, so that you get thinner slices, which are easier to eat. Cut the squid into thin strips, or a single slice if it is tender and not too thick.

MAKES 2 BIG BOWLS

10 oz vinegared rice ($^3/_4$ cup raw rice)

1 boned chicken leg

2 eggs

1 medium carrot

2 tbsp fresh peas

white sesame seeds (optional)

FOR THE TERIYAKI SAUCE:

1 tbsp soy sauce

1 tbsp sake (optional)

$^1/_2$ tbsp mirin (optional)

1 tbsp sugar

1 tbsp water

FOR THE CARROT:

1 tbsp sugar

pinch of salt

$^1/_2$ tsp rice vinegar

4 tbsp water

Mushi-zushi
Steamed sushi

Combine the teriyaki ingredients in a small pan. Bring to a boil and remove from the heat. Let cool. **2.** Make small cuts in the skin of the chicken or the meat if skinless (to allow the teriyaki sauce to soak in). **3.** Put the chicken leg, opened, in a dish and pour sauce over both sides. Set aside. **4.** Peel and cut the carrot in small bite-size pieces. Combine in a small pan with the carrot-cooking liquid and cook on medium heat until they are just tender. **5.** Lightly mix the eggs with a fork or chopsticks. Do not beat or foam. **6.** Heat a nonstick skillet or omelet pan. Pour in the egg while turning the skillet, so that you have a thick layer of egg. As soon as the edges start to dry, flip over and quickly cook the other side. Set aside and repeat until you have used up all the eggs. Set aside to cool. **7.** Cook the peas in boiling water, uncovered. Do not overcook (they should be crisp). **8.** Pre-heat the oven to 400°F and cook the chicken with the teriyaki sauce. Baste regularly with the sauce. When it is nicely browned, remove the chicken from the dish but leave the sauce to keep warm (be careful, the sugar makes the sauce burn). **9.** Boil some water in a double cooker or steamer. **10.** Slice the chicken.

11. In a salad bowl, gently toss together the rice, peas and carrots. **12.** Put the rice mixture in two heat-resistant bowls. **13.** Slice the egg into thin strips. **14.** In each bowl, place half the chicken, some strips of egg, and a few sesame seeds (optional). **15.** As soon as the double boiler or steamer is very hot, place in one or both bowls if possible. **16.** Steam for 5 minutes on high heat. **17.** Take out the bowl (repeat with the second bowl if necessary). **18.** Pour the teriyaki cooking sauce over the chicken only. Cover, if the bowls have lids, and serve hot.

Here the steam doesn't actually cook the food—everything is already cooked anyway—but it makes the different flavors mix together and soak into the rice, and allows the vinegar from the rice to soak into the other ingredients a little. This is a hot sushi—you can use beef, salmon, duck or tofu, and other cooked ingredients instead of chicken.

SERVES 4

10 oz vinegared rice
($\frac{3}{4}$ cup raw rice)

10 oz raw salmon

1–2 lemons
or 2 limes

soy sauce

soy sauce and
wasabi, to serve

plastic wrap

round cake pan,
8 inches in diameter

Remon to namajake no hako-zushi
Hako-zushi of marinated salmon with lemon

Put the salmon in the freezer for 30 minutes before cutting into thin slices. The best technique is to press the fish with one hand while cutting at a 45° angle with the other hand (see "how to cut fish" page 183). **2.** Cut the lemon into thin slices. **3.** Cover the bottom and sides of the round pan with plastic wrap, leaving a generous overlap over the sides. **4.** Start by lining the bottom of the pan, on the wrap, with the slices of lemon, and then line up the slices of salmon, overlapping slightly. **5.** Spread the rice evenly on the salmon with wet fingers, press firmly without squashing the grains of rice. **6.** Close the plastic wrap over everything, press again, this time with the flat bottom of a cup or box, over the wrap so that the rice is compressed. **7.** Chill in the refrigerator for an hour. **8.** Open the plastic wrap. Turn out the sushi on a plate. **9.** Remove the wrap, taking care that the lemon and salmon do not get detached from the rice (if you have pressed firmly at each step, you shouldn't have any trouble). **10.** Cut like a cake with a wet knife and serve with wasabi and soy sauce.

Osumashi
Clear soup

If you use instant dashi (ready-to-use powdered stock, sold in Japanese and some Chinese grocery stores), heat the water and pour in the powder. **2.** If you use *katsuobushi* (dried shaved bonito flakes, sold in Japanese grocery stores), bring the water to a boil and simmer the *katsuobushi* in it for 5 minutes. Filter through a fine sieve lined with muslin so that the stock is perfectly clear. **3.** With any other stock, make sure all the fat has been discarded. Filter well—the liquid should be perfectly clear. **4.** Cut the beans into equal lengths. Cook in boiling water, uncovered. Do not overcook; they should be very crisp. Divide into two bundles. **5.** Cut the chicken into two very thin slices. Wrap a slice around a bundle of the beans. The chicken meat should stick and each bundle should hold by itself. **6.** Heat the water or stock over medium heat. Do not allow to boil. Gently place the bundles of beans and chicken so that they are completely immersed in the stock. Turn the heat down to a very low simmer. When the chicken is cooked (it will whiten), delicately place each bunch in a bowl and pour the stock over it. **7.** Sprinkle with chopped chives, shallots or slivers of carrot.

Miso soup is eaten every day in Japanese families, but osumashi, an elegant, delicate and perfectly clear soup, is served in restaurants. The key to success is the dashi. You can never use too much *katsuobushi* to make the stock. If you prefer, you can replace the chicken and beans with squares of Japanese tofu or small pieces of a white fish such as sea bream or cod.

MAKES 2 JAPANESE SOUP BOWLS

1/3 package instant dashi, or 2 tbsp *katsuobushi*

1 1/4 cups water

1 1/4 cups water, or fat-free chicken, fish or vegetable stock

2 thin slices chicken breast

10 thin green beans

carrot, shallot, chives (optional)

**MAKES 4 JAPANESE
SOUP BOWLS**

1 ³/₄ cups dashi

1–2 tbsp miso

**WHATEVER YOU WANT
TO PUT IN IT:**

tofu

potato

green or white cabbage

onion

mushrooms

Miso-shiru
Miso soup

Heat the dashi (see recipe for osumashi clear soup opposite). Add the ingredient of your choice, cut in strips or in bite-size pieces. Cook on medium heat. **2.** Put the miso paste in a ladle. Plunge it into the stock. While holding the ladle in the pan, gradually dilute the miso by mixing the stock and the miso in the ladle with a spoon. Mix with the dashi. Serve hot.

There are as many different types of miso as there are regions in Japan, if not more. Usually, miso from the Kanto region (Eastern Japan, Tokyo) is red and salty. The miso of the Kansai region (Western Japan, Kyoto, Osaka, Nara) is white and rather sweet. Some miso, such as the one from Nagoya, are very black and salty. The amount of miso to water depends on the dashi (very salty or not). Adjust the amounts of dashi and miso to taste. In Japanese families, miso soup is served practically at every meal. A centuries-old "instant soup" (especially if you use powdered instant dashi), you can add practically any vegetable, meat or fish you like. Japanese tofu doesn't need cooking: it should just be heated. You only have to wait for a few minutes before adding the miso.

SERVES 4

5 eggs

1 tbsp sugar

1 tbsp mirin

pinch of salt

1 tsp peanut or
sunflower oil

$^3/_4$ cup dashi
(optional)

Tamago
Sweet omelet

Tamago is easier to make if you have a square *tamagoyaki* pan, sold in Japanese grocery stores. If you don't, you can use a round or oval nonstick omelet pan or skillet.

1. Mix the eggs with a fork or chopsticks but do not beat or foam. **2.** Add sugar, mirin and salt. Mix and strain. **3.** Heat the pan. Coat with oil using paper towels. **4.** Pour a third of the egg mixture into the pan, turning it to cover the base evenly. **5.** When the egg is half cooked, fold into thirds and push toward the edge of the pan. **6.** Using the same oiled piece of paper towel, apply another coat of oil on the free part of the pan. **7.** Pour half the egg mixture into the free part of the pan. **8.** When it is half cooked, fold the previously cooked and folded layer over it, so that you have a flat rectangular "roll". **9.** Repeat with the rest of the egg mixture.

It's difficult to make a perfectly rectangular *tamagoyaki* such as you may see in sushi restaurants (mine always come out triangular!). The main thing is that the layers should be rolled over each other, without over cooking any of them— they should be soft but not runny. If you only have a round pan, you can cheat a little by cutting the edges off to make it rectangular and eat while still piping hot! Each sushiya has his own jealously guarded recipe. Some add pureed shrimp or fish. I sometimes add dashi (bonito stock).

MAKES 3 FUTOMAKI

1¼ lb vinegared rice
(1½ cups raw rice)

4½ sheets nori
(1½ sheets per maki)

makisu

Futomaki-zushi
Thick roll

A real futomaki is hard work. You have to make each of the five fillings. This recipe is made with traditional ingredients that you will only find in Japanese or some Chinese grocery stores. But you are always free to try other ingredients.

Sweet shiitake mushrooms

8 big and thick, dried shiitake mushrooms

½ package of instant dashi

3 tbsp sugar

1½ tbsp mirin

2 tbsp soy sauce

1. Wash the mushrooms under the tap. Place in a pan, cover with water and let soak until soft. Discard the stems. **2.** Add the dashi and sugar but do not discard or change the water. Cook on medium heat for 3 to 4 minutes. **3.** Skim and add mirin and soy sauce. **4.** Simmer on low heat until just tender. **5.** Cut the shiitake mushrooms into slices, ⅛–¼ inch thick.

Kanpyo

12 strips kanpyo, 5 inches long

¾ cup dashi
or ½ package instant dashi
in ¾ cup water

3 tbsp sugar

1½ tbsp mirin

2 tbsp soy sauce

1. Wash the kanpyo strips under the tap. **2.** Place them in a large bowl and knead them with salt to break the fiber. **3.** Rinse and cover with cold water. Set aside to soak for at least 1 hour. **4.** Boil in the same water until they are tender but crisp. Rinse in cold water. **5.** Mix the dashi and sugar in a pan. Add the kanpyo. **6.** Cook over medium heat for 3 to 4 minutes. Add the mirin and soy sauce. Cover with a lid smaller than the pan, so that it rests directly on the kanpyo. **7.** Cook until all the liquid is absorbed. **8.** Spread the kanpyo on a cutting board and let cool.

Tamago-yaki
See pages 104–105

Spinach
Wash and boil spinach in a little water, stirring to make
sure it doesn't stick. Drain thoroughly and blot dry with
paper towels.

Beni shoga
(red ginger)
Cut red ginger into small thin strips.
It is sold in packets or jars.

Technique for Futomaki
1. Place the whole sheet of nori on the makisu towards you and
lengthen it by placing a half sheet above it, slightly overlapping.
2. Spread the rice on the nori, leaving 1/2 inch above and below
the nori uncovered. **3.** With 2 wet fingers, dig 5 grooves, starting
from the center of the rice, of about 1 1/4 inches apart. **4.** Place an
ingredient lengthwise in each groove. **5.** Lift the side of the makisu
that is nearest you with both thumbs and hold the ingredients with
the tips of the other fingers. Roll. **6.** Keep rolling while pressing
firmly, until the nori is completely folded into itself. Do not be afraid
of breaking or squashing the roll. **7.** Without unrolling the makisu
and with your palms on each side of the roll, tuck in the rice and
other ingredients that have spread out from the sides of the roll.
8. Unroll the makisu. Cut the futomaki with a wet knife, which you
must wipe with a damp cloth after each cut.

Cook the tiger shrimp in boiling water until it turns pink. Let cool and peel. Cut into 3 pieces (2 if it is small). **2.** Put the clams in a pan but do not add any liquid. Cover and cook over moderate heat, shaking the pan, until they open. (Discard any that do not open.) Let cool and shell. **3.** Cut the sea-urchin open with scissors and take out the meat with a small spoon (only the dark red meat, not the liquid and grainy matter). **4.** Open the scallop. Usually, only the adductor muscle is eaten (the thick round white meat), but you can also use the other parts if you like. Clean whatever you are keeping with paper towels and set aside. **5.** In a small bowl or dish (here, the lower shell of a scallop has been used), place the rice and gently press with wet fingers, without squashing it. **6.** Place the shrimp, sea urchin, scallop and clams on the rice. Tear the nori into little pieces and scatter over the seafood. **7.** Serve with wasabi and soy sauce, if desired.

MAKES 1

5 oz vinegared rice
(⅓ cup raw rice)

1 big tiger shrimp

1 sea-urchin

2 scallops

2 small clams

1 tsp salmon roe

¼ sheet nori

wasabi
(optional)

soy sauce
(optional)

Gyokai-rui no chirashi
Seafood chirashi

SERVES 4

2 lb vinegared rice
(2 1/4 cups raw rice)

1 can crab meat

5 surimi sticks

1 ball mozzarella

2 spears green
asparagus
or 1/2 avocado

1 hard-cooked egg
(optional)

few sprigs dill
(optional)

Kani no chirashi

Crab chirashi

Cook the asparagus, uncovered, in boiling water until just tender, or peel and cut the avocado in long strips. **2.** With the tips of your fingers, tear the mozzarella into strips. **3.** Open the can of crab and drain thoroughly. **4.** Squeeze the sticks of surimi between your fingers to break them into strips. **5.** Mash the hard-cooked egg yolk with a fork (if using). **6.** Toss everything together with the vinegared rice. **7.** Cover and let rest in a cool place, but do not refrigerate. **8.** Serve garnished with dill sprigs, if desired.

Temari-zushi
Tuna, salmon and flounder temari-zushi

Cut the fish in thin slices. **2.** Wet your hands and form 9 rice balls. **3.** Take a piece of plastic wrap, about 5-inches square, in the palm of your hand. Place a sprig of dill in the center (optional). **4.** Place one or two slices of fish on it (do not mix different fish). Dab a little wasabi on top (optional). **5.** Place a ball of rice on the fish slice and wasabi (if using) and close your hand over everything. **6.** Twist the plastic wrap so that you have a tight package. Press this ball in your hand. **7.** Open and remove the wrap. **8.** Repeat steps 3–7 nine times with different fish. Garnish as you like.

It's difficult to buy such small quantities of fish, and even if you have talked your fishman into it, you will still have the problem of cutting such small-size fish into thin slices. Make it easy for yourself and buy only one fish (except if you are making a lot of temari-zushi), such as salmon, flounder, sea bream... have your fishman fillet it, which you can then slice thinly. As for rest of the fish, often untidy bits and pieces, you can use them to make maki (see recipe for Tuna and spring onion maki on page 134). You will then have a nice platter with two types of sushi.

**MAKES 9
TEMARI-ZUSHI**

10 oz vinegared rice
($^3/_4$ cup raw rice)

1–1$^1/_2$ oz tuna

1–1$^1/_2$ oz salmon

1–1$^1/_2$ oz flounder

few sprigs dill
(optional)

wasabi
(optional)

soy sauce
(optional)

plastic wrap

MAKES 1 OSHI-ZUSHI

10 oz vinegared rice
($^3/_4$ cup raw rice)

$3^1/_2$ oz salmon

$3^1/_2$ oz flounder

3 pinches of salt
(optional)

few sprigs dill,
for garnish (optional)

soy sauce

plastic wrap

rectangular cake pan
or any box approx.
8 x 4 inches

Sake to hirame no oshi-zushi

Oshi-zushi of salmon and flounder

Put the fish in the refrigerator for 30 minutes to firm up before cutting. Cut the salmon and flounder in slices $^1/_8$ inch thick. **2.** Salt the flounder and let drain for about 10 minutes in a strainer. Gently wipe off the salt with paper towels. **3.** Cover the bottom and sides of the pan with plastic wrap. It should be twice as big as the pan and overlap generously over the sides. **4.** On top of the wrap, in the bottom of the pan, press half of the rice in a thick layer. **5.** Layer half of the fish onto the rice, alternating a slice of salmon with a slice of flounder and so on. **6.** Spread the remaining rice over the fish. **7.** Layer the rest of the salmon and flounder as before. Try not to leave any gaps. If necessary, cut the fish so that all the gaps are filled. **8.** Close the wrap tightly. **9.** Press over everything with a rectangular object, smaller than the pan. Press very firmly. Do not be afraid to squash. **10.** Let the sushi rest in the refrigerator for an hour, without unwrapping. **11.** Take the sushi out of the pan and discard the wrap. **12.** Cut with a wet knife, which must be wiped with a damp cloth after each cut. **13.** Garnish with a few sprigs of dill, or the garnish of your choice, and serve in a dish with wasabi and soy sauce.

SERVES 1

5 oz vinegared rice
($^1/_3$ cup raw rice)

$^1/_2$ medium cucumber

1 tbsp salt

TOPPINGS, TO TASTE:

sea-urchin,
squid, sliced into strips,
salmon roe,
white tuna with
mayonnaise,
crab meat,
small shrimp, etc.

soy sauce
(optional)

wasabi
(optional)

Kyuri no gunkan-maki
Cucumber gunkan-maki

Wash and peel the cucumber, leaving on some skin for color. **2.** Take some salt in your hands and knead the cucumber with it. Let rest for an hour. **3.** Rinse the cucumber and dry with paper towels. Cut into 1–1$^1/_4$-inch pieces. **4.** Seed each piece with a small spoon. **5.** Fill each piece with vinegared rice, to about $^2/_3$ of its height. Fill in with the topping ingredient of your choice. **6.** Serve with wasabi and soy sauce.

Genmai no chirashi

Whole rice vegetarian chirashi

Soak the rice in the water for at least an hour. **2.** Cook the bamboo in boiling water for a few minutes, drain and mince. **3.** Cut the mushrooms and carrot in small pieces. **4.** Cook the vegetables so that they are just tender but crunchy in the vegetable cooking mixture. Drain. **5.** Cook the rice in the water in which it has been soaking, following the cooking method described on page 185. **6.** Heat the *awasezu* ingredients without boiling, and remove from the heat as soon as the sugar has melted. When the rice is cooked, pour the *awasezu* over it while "cutting" with a wet wooden spatula (see page 185). Quickly mix in the vegetables. **7.** If you wish to add nori, cut it into thin strips with scissors, and scatter over the rice. **8.** Serve warm.

You can add fried tofu cut into bite size pieces. If you buy it ready-fried, dip it in boiling water for a few seconds to get rid of excess fat. You can also use Chinese tofu (firmer than Japanese), slice it thin or thick, to taste, and grill the slices with a little soy sauce.

SERVES 4

1$\frac{1}{4}$ lb raw whole rice

4 cups water

1 package bamboo shoots, or 1 medium can

6 mushrooms

1 carrot

4 shiitake mushrooms

1 tbsp fresh peas

AWASEZU
(RICE FLAVORING):

3 tbsp rice vinegar

2 tsp sugar

1 tsp salt

TO COOK THE VEGETA-BLES:

8 cups dashi or water

$\frac{1}{2}$ tsp sugar

$\frac{1}{2}$ tsp salt

$\frac{1}{2}$ tbsp sake

$\frac{1}{2}$ sheet nori (optional)

MAKES 6 TO 8 SLICES

1 medium squid

1 egg

1 tbsp fresh peas

1–2 pinches of salt

soy sauce

wasabi

AWASEZU
(VINEGAR MIX):

4 tbsp rice vinegar

1½ tbsp sugar

large pinch of salt

Prepare the *awasezu* by combining the ingredients in a large bowl. **2.** If you are using ready-to-use or frozen squid, go directly to step 7. You can make this recipe with or without the tentacles. **3.** Separate the tentacles and the body of the squid by pulling gently but firmly.

Ika-zushi

Squid sushi

4. Cut the tentacles just below the eyes. Set aside. **5.** Empty and clean the body completely. **6.** Wash it under the tap, inside and out, and scratch off the thin skin of the body with your fingers. Also wash the tentacles. **7.** Drop the tentacles and body into a pan of boiling salted water. Watch out for the moment when the tentacles start to curl, when their color changes, and when the body rounds as this indicates that it is done. Do not overcook otherwise it will be tough. Drain on paper towels. **8.** Without letting it cool, soak immediately in the *awasezu* and leave to marinate while you prepare the filling. **9.** Mix the egg without beating or foaming, with a fork or chopsticks. **10.** Pour the egg into a nonstick omelet pan or skillet, turning it to coat with a thin layer of egg (it doesn't matter if the layer is uneven). **11.** Cut the cooked egg in thin strips. **12.** Cook the peas in boiling water, uncovered. Do not overcook; they should be crisp. **13.** Take the squid out of the *awasezu* and cut half of the tentacles into very small pieces. **14.** In a large bowl, toss together the rice, tentacle pieces, peas and the egg strips.

15. With a spoon, stuff this mixture into the body of the squid. Do not be afraid of squashing the rice: it's better squashed, it will make it easier to cut. **16.** Let rest for a few hours in a cool place. If the room is too hot, wrap the squid tightly in plastic wrap before refrigerating. **17.** Cut with a wet knife and serve with wasabi and soy sauce.

Ika in Japanese means squid. When choosing squid, pick one that is bright eyed, with a firm texture and a slight smell of iodine. You can also use squid that is already cleaned and ready to use. But choose carefully—it should be white and not yellowish. If using frozen squid, make sure it is completely thawed before cooking.

MAKES 6 "POUCHES"

10 oz vinegared rice
($^{3}/_{4}$ cup raw rice)

6 eggs

pinch of salt

1 tsp sugar

$^{1}/_{3}$ tsp cornstarch

1 tsp white
sesame seeds

$^{1}/_{2}$ medium carrot

2–3 small
cooked shrimp

green peas

few sprigs of parsley,
with long stems

Fukusa-zushi
Sushi egg wraps

A *fukusa* is a square of doubled silk used during the tea ceremony to delicately wipe the cups or to wrap things in.

1. Mix the eggs, salt, sugar, and cornstarch, without beating or foaming, with a fork or chopsticks. Divide into 6 portions. **2.** Spray or coat a nonstick omelet pan or skillet with a drop of oil. Pour one portion of the egg mixture in the center of the skillet and turn it to spread thinly, making a thin sheet of egg. **3.** As soon as the surface of the egg is almost dry, gently turn and quickly cook the other side. Do not brown. The sheet of egg should be yellow. Make a further 5 sheets with the remaining egg portions. Set aside to cool. **4.** Peel and cook the carrot whole, either in boiling water or steamed. Chop very finely. **5.** With a wet wooden spatula, gently mix together the carrot and sesame with the rice, without squashing the rice. Set aside. **6.** Wet your hands and form 6 round rice balls, trying not to squash the rice too much (a little bit of squashing is ok). **7.** Dip the parsley stems in boiling water for a few seconds. **8.** Take an "egg sheet" in the hollow of your hand. **9.** Place a ball of rice in the middle of the sheet, in the hollow of your hand. **10.** Close the egg sheet around the rice. Tie a parsley stem around it to close the package. **11.** Arrange the folds of the egg to make a nice-looking pouch. **12.** Decorate each pouch with a shrimp or a few peas in the opening.

**MAKES 1 *SUEHIROMAKI*
OR *TEMAKI***

2 oz vinegared rice
(2 tbsp raw rice)

¼ or ½ sheet nori

1 or 2 slices avocado

1 stick surimi

1 lettuce leaf,
green part only
(round or batavia is best)

1 tsp mayonnaise

MAKES 1 MAKI

5 oz vinegared rice
(⅓ cup raw rice)

⅔ sheet nori

2 slices avocado

2 sticks surimi

1 lettuce leaf,
green part only
(round or batavia is best)

1 tsp mayonnaise

**MAKES 1 *URAMAKI*
("INSIDE-OUT" MAKI)**

150 g (5 oz)
vinegared rice
(75 g/2½ oz raw rice)

1 sheet nori

2 slices avocado

2 sticks surimi

1 lettuce leaf,
green part only
(round or batavia is best)

1 tsp mayonnaise

1 tbsp white
sesame seeds

makisu

plastic wrap

small cutting board

For the *suehiromaki* or *temaki*: **1.** Place a square sheet of nori in your left hand, one corner pointing downward. **2.** Place a heaped tablespoonful of rice in the center of the nori, vertically. **3.** Place the filling in the middle of the rice, lengthwise. **4.** Roll into a cone by folding over the left and right sides of the nori.

Kariforunia roru
California roll

For the maki: 1. Place the nori on the makisu. **2.** Spread the rice on the nori, about ½-inch thick, leaving about ½ inch border of nori at the top and bottom. **3.** Tear the lettuce leaf into small pieces and line up the pieces horizontally across the rice, making a continuous strip of green down the middle of the rice. **4.** Place the avocado and surimi sticks on the lettuce. **5.** Spread the mayonnaise on the surimi. **6.** Lift the edge of the makisu nearest to you with both thumbs, holding the avocado and surimi in place with the tips of the other fingers. Roll carefully but tightly. When the roll is almost complete, press several times all over the makisu. Then complete the roll, pressing again, even more firmly this time. Do not be afraid to press hard, even if some mayonnaise squishes out from the sides! **7.** Unroll the makisu. Cut the roll into thick slices with a very sharp knife wiped with a damp cloth after each cut.

For the "inside out" maki (*uramaki*): 1. Place a sheet of nori on the board and spread rice over it with fingers, about ½ inch thick. **2.** Sprinkle sesame seeds over the rice. Tap with your fingers to make sure the sesame has stuck to the rice. **3.** Cover with plastic wrap—it should be bigger than the nori.

4. Place the makisu on the wrap. **5.** Quickly but carefully invert the board with everything on it. Now the makisu is underneath and the nori on top. **6.** Place the lettuce leaf, avocado and surimi, with a little mayonnaise, horizontally down the middle of the nori. **7.** Roll while holding the wrap in place. Be careful, at the end of the rolling motion, that the rice is completely folded into itself, wrapping in the lettuce, avocado and surimi in the middle. The rice acts like a glue and closes the roll. **8.** Press very firmly, so that the sesame is really stuck in the rice and the roll is very tight. **9.** Unroll the makisu and the wrap. **10.** Cut into thick slices with a wet knife, wiping the blade with a damp cloth after each cut.

See page 187 "How to make maki" for more detail on rolling. Uramaki sounds complicated but it's actually fairly easy. You just need to practice a bit—your first rolls will tend to be "cone shaped" because you won't roll straight, or fall apart before or after cutting. That's because most people are afraid to press firmly while rolling. Don't wait until you have rolled it completely to press, but start rolling, stop, press, roll a bit more, stop, press, finish rolling, stop, press... you can always tuck in the sides or cut them off and eat them by yourself in the kitchen!

MAKES 1 HAKO-ZUSHI

5 oz vinegared rice
(1/3 cup raw rice)

1 or 2 large slices
smoked salmon

1 tbsp salmon roe

few sprigs of dill

soy sauce
(optional)

plastic wrap

muffin pan or small
round box, approx.
1 3/4 inches high,
with a flat bottom

Sumoku samon no hako-zushi

Hako-zushi of smoked salmon

Line the muffin pan or box with plastic wrap, letting the edges drape generously over the sides. **2.** Line the bottom and the sides of the pan with slices of smoked salmon, cut in long wide strips. They should overlap slightly to cover the bottom evenly. **3.** Make sure that you cut the strips long enough so you can fold them over the rice once the pan is full. **4.** Pour half the rice into the pan onto the salmon and press lightly with wet fingers. Sprinkle some dill over the surface. **5.** Pour in the rest of the rice and press lightly. **6.** Fold the salmon strips over the rice and press down firmly. **7.** Fold the wrap over the top. Remove from the pan and gently press together in your hands on all sides. **8.** Set aside in a cool place. **9.** Take off the wrap, place on a dish and decorate with salmon roe and dill.

In Japanese, *hako* means "box." In fact, any box will do; if you use a big box, you can cut your sushi in little squares. You can place thin slices of lemon on the salmon before folding the wrap over it. If you want a change from fish, you can use roast beef or ham cut in very thin slices, replacing the dill with minced pickles or capers. Serve with lemon, shoyu, wasabi, horseradish, grated fresh ginger, mayonnaise... experiment and enjoy!

SERVES 2

10 oz vinegared rice
($^3/_4$ cup raw rice)

5 oz tuna

1 fillet of sea bream

$^1/_2$ sheet nori

1 tbsp salmon roe

few scallions

$^1/_2$ tsp sake
(optional)

2 green asparagus
spears (optional)

$^1/_4$ cucumber
(optional)

white sesame seeds
(optional)

wasabi
(optional)

soy sauce

pickled ginger
(see page 50)

Edo no chirashi

Chirashi of Edo

Cook the asparagus in boiling water, uncovered. **2.** Cut the cucumber into thin slices. **3.** Cut the tuna in bite-size pieces. **4.** Thinly slice the sea bream. **5.** Pour a few drops of sake on the salmon roe and mix gently (optional). **6.** Slice the scallions very finely. **7.** Tear the nori and mix it quickly with the rice. Put the rice mixture in a lacquered box, a bowl or a deep soup plate. **8.** Place the tuna and sea bream on half the surface of the rice, sprinkle the other half with salmon roe, scallions, and sesame seeds. **9.** Serve with soy sauce and pickled ginger, and wasabi if desired.

Don't forget to feast your eyes—fish with contrasting colors look better than fish of same color tones. Match strong-tasting fish with delicate-tasting fish. For example, tuna and sole, tuna and sea bream, salmon and sole, sea bream and fresh mackerel, tuna and squid, tuna and sea bass. Avoid putting salmon and tuna together.

Combine the ingredients for the vinaigrette. **2.** Slice the top off the bell pepper, so that the top part makes a lid. Scoop out the inside. **3.** Cut the onion in thin half rings. Rinse under the tap and drain well. **4.** Cook the chicken breast in boiling water. Tear into strips with your fingers. **5.** In a bowl, combine the rice, chicken, onion and dressing. Fill the bell pepper with this mixture. **6.** Garnish with sprigs of cilantro.

The bell pepper is only a substitute for a pretty bowl. You can use any bowl or cup.

Chuka-fu chirashi
Chinese chirashi

SERVES 1

5 oz vinagared rice
($\frac{1}{3}$ cup raw rice)

1 oz chicken breast meat

$\frac{1}{8}$ red onion

few sprigs cilantro

1 large bell pepper,
(yellow, orange or red)

FOR THE VINAIGRETTE:

2 tsp soy sauce

$\frac{1}{4}$ tsp sesame oil

2 tsp rice vinegar

1 tsp sugar

2 tsp sunflower oil

$\frac{1}{2}$ tsp white
sesame seeds

pinch of salt

few sprigs of
cilantro

MAKES 1 ORANGE

3$\frac{1}{2}$ oz vinegared rice
($\frac{1}{4}$ cup raw rice)

$\frac{1}{2}$ tbsp salmon roe

$\frac{1}{2}$ tbsp fresh peas

pinch of salt

1 large orange

Orenji-kappu-zushi

Orange cup sushi

Choose a nice big round orange. Cut off and retain the top to use as a lid. **2.** Scoop out the orange, scraping everything away with a spoon. **3.** Let it dry. **4.** Cook the peas in boiling water, with a pinch of salt, uncovered. Let cool. **5.** Combine the rice and peas in a bowl. **6.** Fill the orange with the rice mixture. Place some salmon roe on top of the rice. **7.** Serve with the lid and a small spoon.

You can use lemon instead of orange, or a grapefruit. However, orange is best suited to this recipe, because its color is close to that of salmon roe. The orange also gives a pleasant fragrance to the sushi.

Tokyo no tekkadon
Tekkadon of Tokyo

MAKES 1 LARGE BOWL

5 oz vinegared rice
(^{1}/$_3$ cup raw rice)

1 sheet nori

3^1/$_2$–5 oz tuna

wasabi
(optional)

soy sauce

Cut the tuna in small bite-size pieces, about ³/₄–1 inch, and ½ inch thick. **2.** Fold the nori four times, then cut into thin strips with scissors. **3.** Place the rice in a large bowl. **4.** Top with the tuna, followed by the nori. **5.** Add, if you wish, a small ball of wasabi. **6.** Serve with soy sauce.

In theory, *tekkadon* ("bowl of red iron") should be made with red tuna, but you can also use toro, salmon, or any other strong tasting fish. Serve with miso soup, and you will have a complete meal, easy and very delicious.

129

T H E   R E C I P E S

Nigiri-zushi

Assorted nigiri

Cut the fish into slices about ⅓ inch thick for the tuna and salmon; ⅛–¼ inch for the white fish and mackerel. **2.** Butterfly-cut the scallop (cut nearly in half lengthwise but not completely; one side stays attached; spread open) so that each scallop is shaped like a figure 8. **3.** For the mackerel, follow the instructions for bo-zushi of mackerel on page 141. **4.** Cook the octopus beforehand so that it has the time to cool, for about 15 minutes in boiling water with 2 pinches of salt. **5.** Choose a medium-size squid, not too thick. Thick squid may be difficult to chew. **6.** To make nigiri, follow the instructions on page 186. **7.** Serve accompanied by soy sauce, pickled ginger and wasabi, if desired.

MAKES AN ASSORTMENT FOR 1

¾ oz vinegared rice (2 tsp raw rice) per nigiri

tuna

salmon

sea bream

sea bass

flounder

marinated mackerel (see page 141)

1 tiger shrimp

tamago (see page 104)

octopus (tentacle) or squid

scallop

sea urchin

salmon roe

pickled ginger (see page 50)

soy sauce

wasabi (optional)

MAKES 6 GUNKAN-MAKI

4 oz vinegared rice
($\frac{1}{4}$ cup raw rice)

$\frac{1}{2}$ sheet nori

wasabi (optional)

soy sauce

TOPPINGS, TO TASTE:

small shrimp

salmon roe

lumpfish roe

white tuna with
mayonnaise

crabmeat

finely chopped
smoked herring
with cottage cheese

sea urchin, etc.

Gunkan-maki no moriawase

Assorted gunkan-maki

Roast the nori by passing it quickly in a sweeping motion over high heat, both sides. Do not burn: the purpose is to make it crisp, not to cook. **2.** Cut the half sheet of nori into 1$\frac{1}{4}$-inch wide strips. **3.** Wet your hands, take some rice and make an oval-shaped ball of rice about $\frac{3}{4}$ inch high. Set aside and repeat, wetting your hands each time. **4.** Wrap a strip of nori around each rice ball, like a belt. It should stick. If you have trouble "sealing" the nori, you can cheat and stick one side of the nori to the other with a grain of rice. Top with the ingredient of your choice with a small spoon. The nori, which makes a sort of high edge, should hold the garnish in place. **5.** Place a dot of wasabi on each sushi (optional). **6.** Serve with soy sauce.

Gunkan-maki is suited to all garnishes that contain mayonnaise, cottage cheese and sauce, as well as salmon and lumpfish roe, in fact, any ingredient that is wet or liquid. A good trick to remember: the nori should be about $\frac{1}{4}$ inch higher than the rice ball.

SERVES 2

1 lb vinegared rice
(1¼ cups raw rice)

3 sheets nori

¾ oz red tuna

¾ oz salmon

1 small can
white tuna

⅛ avocado

¼ medium cucumber

1 stick surimi

1 tsp mayonnaise

French mustard
(optional)

wasabi
(optional)

soy sauce

makisu

Hoso-maki no moriawase
Assorted hoso-maki

Cut the fillings into thin sticks. Seed and peel the cucumber. (With organic cucumber, you may leave the skin, if you wish.) Combine the white tuna with the mayonnaise, or prepare a more tangy mixture with a half teaspoon each of mustard and mayonnaise. **2.** Cut each sheet of nori in two (half a sheet for each sushi ingredient). **3.** Following the technique for rolling maki described on page 187, spread a thin layer of rice on a half sheet of nori, without squashing the grains of rice. Leave a border of nori of about ½ inch at the top and bottom of the sheet. Dig a groove horizontally across the center of the rice. **4.** If you wish, spread a little wasabi on the rice. **5.** Place the filling in the groove in an uninterrupted line. **6.** Lift the edges of the makisu with both thumbs and roll it delicately, holding the filling in place with the tips of your fingers. Roll firmly. **7.** Press firmly over the whole length of the makisu. Repeat the operation with the other ingredients. **8.** Cut each roll into 6 or 8 pieces with a wet knife which you must wipe with a damp cloth after each cut.

Hoso-maki means "thin roll." It's the basic maki, the one you see in all sushi restaurants. You can roll whatever you wish: red tuna, toro, salmon, carrot, white tuna, crab meat, salad, beef, grilled or teriyaki chicken, shrimp, cooked eel, etc. You can find ready-to-use cooked eel (commonly referred to as "eel" although it is actually conger) in Japanese grocery stores where they are sold frozen or vacuum packed, since it is practically impossible to make at home from scratch. Raw fish, other than tuna and salmon, do not go very well with maki. The trick to success is to cut the filling of your choice thin enough that you can make tight rolls, but not too thin that you can't taste anything.

Negi-toro-maki
Fatty tuna and scallion roll

Cut the tuna in small pieces and chop finely by tapping it with the blade of a knife. Do not use an electric knife. **2.** Finely chop the scallions and combine with the tuna. **3.** Place a sheet of nori on the makisu. Spread the rice over it, leaving a ½-inch border of nori at top and bottom. **4.** Wet the tips of your fingers and dig a groove horizontally across the center of the layer of rice. **5.** Spread some wasabi into the groove (optional). **6.** Spread some of the tuna mixture evenly into the groove. **7.** Lift the edge of the makisu which is nearest to you with both thumbs and roll firmly while holding the tuna in place with the tips of your other fingers. Press firmly over the entire length of the makisu. **8.** Cut the roll into 6 or 8 pieces with a wet knife, which must be wiped after each cut with a damp cloth to clean off any bits of rice sticking to it. **9.** Serve with pickled ginger and soy sauce.

You can replace the raw tuna by practically any fish, even canned tuna or crab, to which you can add some mayonnaise or mustard. You can also use up the bits of fish left over from the other recipes.

MAKES 2 ROLLS

10 oz vinegared rice
(¾ cup raw rice)

1 sheet nori

3½ oz fatty tuna

2 oz or more,
scallions or chives

wasabi
(optional)

pickled ginger
(optional),
see recipe page 50

makisu

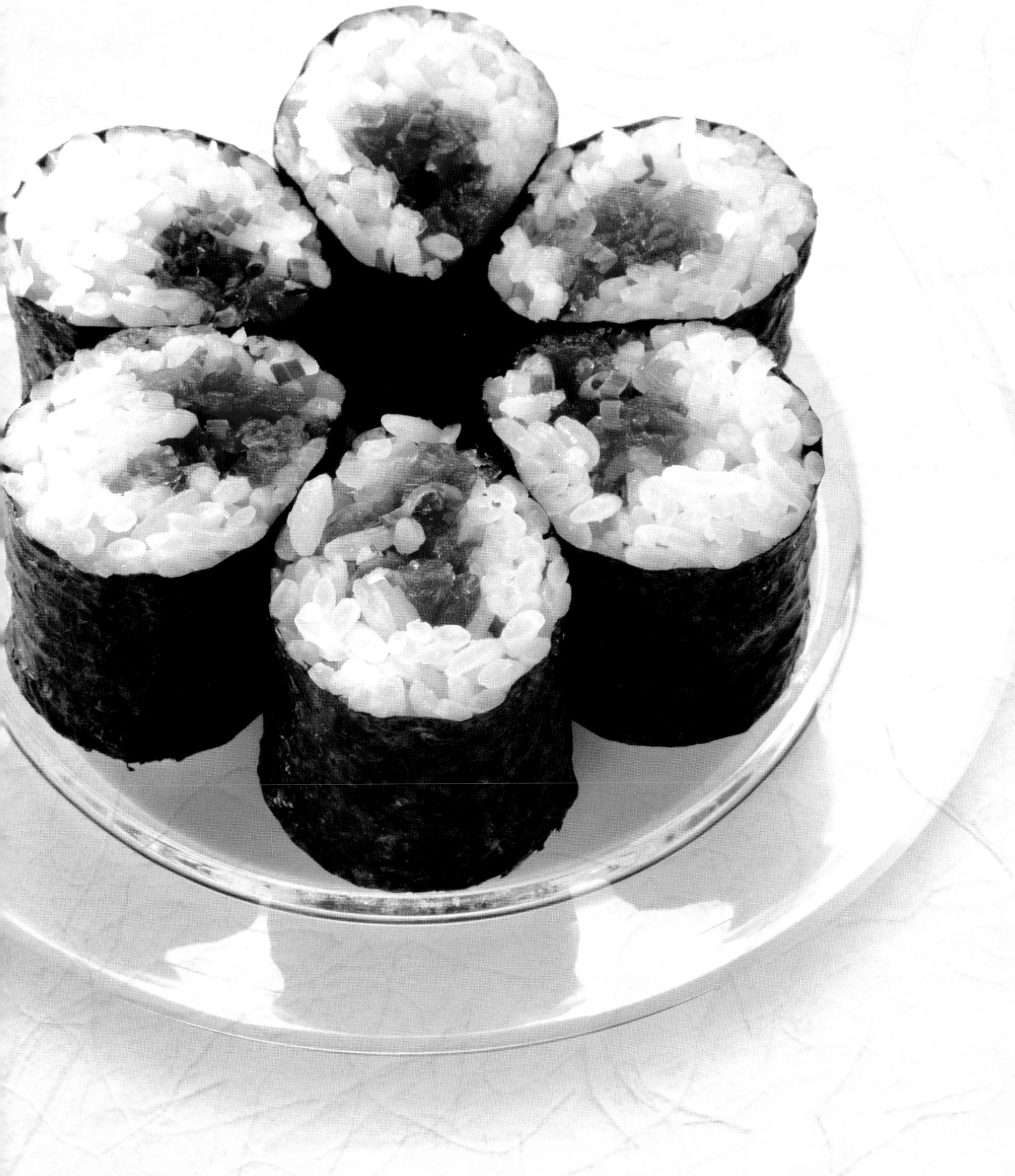

7 oz vinegared rice
(½ cup raw rice)

at least 4 sheets
of nori per person

tuna

salmon

sea bream

shrimp

surimi

tamago
(see pages 104–105)

green asparagus spears

avocado

snowpeas

salmon roe

scallops

white tuna

crabmeat

lumpfish roe

green beans

1 tsp mayonnaise per
small can of tuna or crab

chives, thinly sliced
(optional)

wasabi

soy sauce

pickled ginger
(see page 50, optional)

Te-maki-zushi
Hand roll or "roll-it-yourself" sushi

Te-maki is sushi that you roll yourself, with as much filling as you like (within reason)—a sort of do-it-yourself meal. In Japan it is a common family food—the fishman cuts the fish and seafood to order. All you have to do is prepare the rice, cut the nori and lay everything out attractively on trays or plates. It's practical and a lot of fun.

1. Cut the fillings into easy-to-roll medium-sized thin sticks. **2.** Ask your fishman to fillet the fish. Brush your fingers over the surface of the fish to feel the pin bones and remove them with tweezers. Skin the fish (see "How to cut fish" on page 183). **3.** Cook the vegetables (asparagus, green beans, etc.) uncovered in boiling water. Do not overcook. They should be crisp. Cut them diagonally, it's prettier. **4.** Some ingredients like scallops can't be cut into sticks, so slice them thinly. **5.** Wet ingredients (salmon roe, lumpfish roe, white tuna with mayonnaise, crab, etc.) can be heaped into bowls with teaspoons to serve.

At first, people tend to make big fat te-maki, impossible to roll without some of the food dropping out. It's human to want to make nice straight rolls, but it's easier to make them cone shaped. Some greedy people tend to stuff their rolls too much and end up with fat dynamite sticks that explode in the soy sauce. Each person can experiment as he or she goes. You will laugh, admire well-formed rolls, eat and have fun. You can have some miso or clear soup ready to round up this friendly meal.

SERVES 4

2 lb vinegared rice
(2¼ cups raw rice)

4 large tiger shrimp
or 6 medium

1 medium squid

octopus,
1 big tentacle

4 cherry tomatoes

6 black olives

1 lemon

6 pinches of salt

basil
(optional)

Italian chirashi

Italian chirashi

Cook the shrimp in boiling water with 2 pinches of salt. Drain and peel. **2.** Clean the squid and cook both the body and tentacles in boiling water with 2 pinches of salt (see recipe for Ikazushi, squid sushi, pages 116–117). Drain and set aside. **3.** Cook the tentacle of the octopus for 15 minutes in boiling water with 2 pinches of salt (if the tentacle is thick, knead it with salt and rinse before cooking). Drain and set aside. **4.** Roughly chop the olives. **5.** Cut the shrimp into fairly large pieces and the squid tentacles into small pieces. Cut the squid body into thin circles. Cut the cherry tomatoes into quarters. **6.** Squeeze the lemon and combine the juice with the seafood, tomatoes and olives. Add some basil if you wish. **7.** Toss together with the vinegared rice. **8.** Serve in a large salad bowl.

Suehiro-maki
Cone-shaped sushi

Preparation: if you use green beans or asparagus, cook in boiling water, uncovered. Do not overcook. They should be crisp. Peel and cut the avocado and cucumber into medium-sized thin strips. If you are using herring roe, soak in water for at least 3 hours (overnight is better) to get rid of the salt.

Technique: 1. Take a ¼ sheet of nori in the palm of one hand, one corner pointing downward. **2.** Place a heaped tablespoon of vinegared rice in the center. **3.** In the centre of the rice vertically place a shrimp and a strip of cucumber. Fold the right and left corners of the nori to form a cone, wrapping the filling and leaving it peeping out of the top. **4.** Serve with soy sauce—and wasabi, if desired.

Suehiro-maki is also known as te-maki ("hand roll"). You can use the filling of your choice, as long as you can easily bite into it and it can be cut into sticks. But you can also use white tuna with mayonnaise or red tuna with scallions (see recipe for Tuna and scallion maki on page 134). If you use a fish such as salmon, it's better to chop it very finely so that it's easier to eat.

**MAKES 2
SUEHIRO-MAKI**

3½ oz vinegared rice
(¼ cup raw rice)

½ sheet nori

wasabi
(optional)

soy sauce

FILLINGS, TO TASTE:

large tiger shrimp

crabmeat or surimi

salmon roe

herring roe

green beans

green asparagus spears

avocado

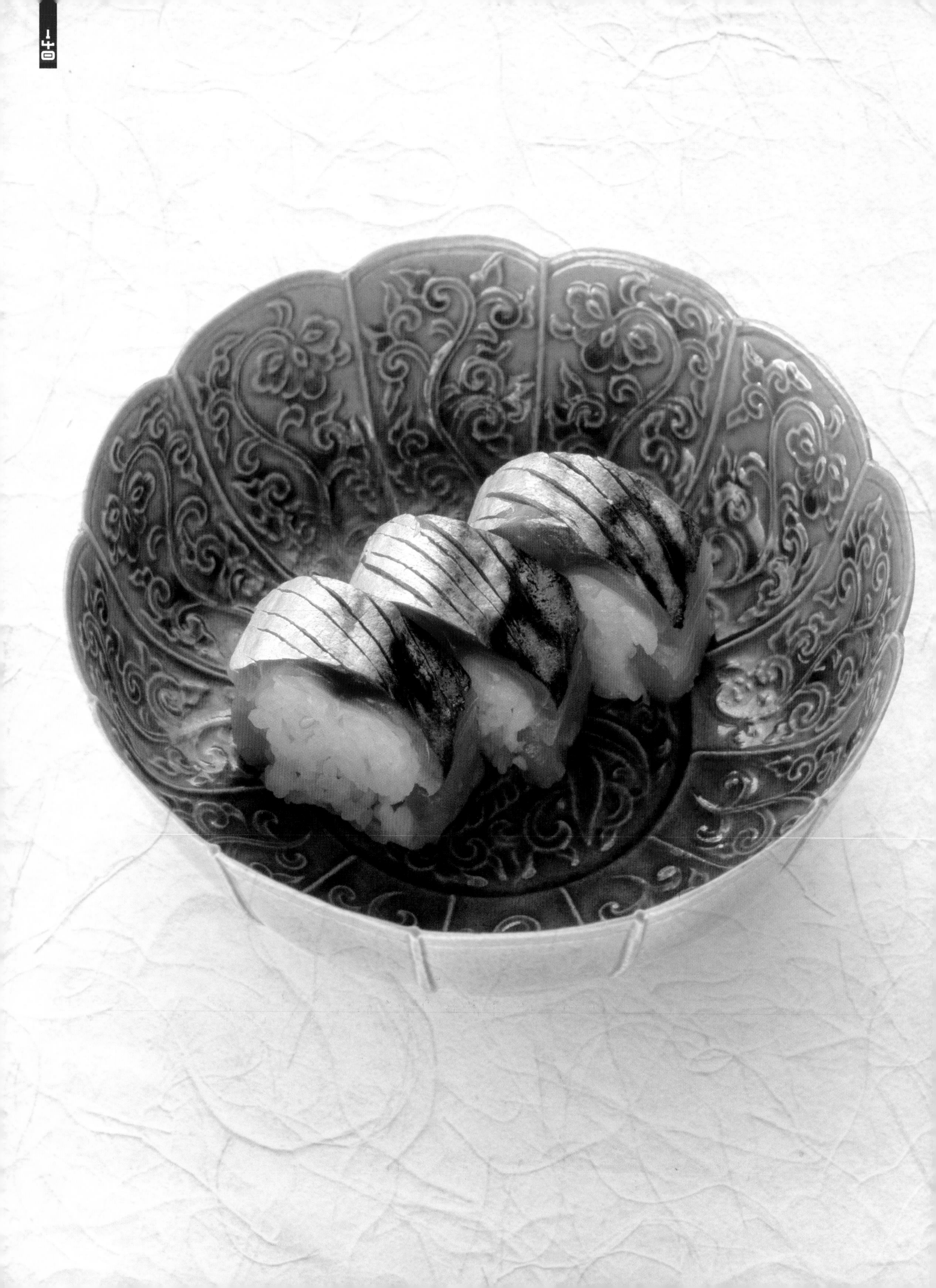

MAKES 2 ROLLS

10 oz vinegared rice
(³⁄₄ cup raw rice)

1–2 mackerel
 fillets

6–7 pinches
of salt per fillet

rice vinegar

wasabi
(optional)

freshly grated ginger

soy sauce

makisu

tweezers

plastic wrap

Saba no bo-zushi

Marinated mackerel bo-zushi

The day before: 1. Ask your fishman to fillet very fresh mackerel without skinning. **2.** Brush your fingers across the surface of the fish—if you feel pin bones, remove them with tweezers. **3.** Salt both sides (flesh and skin). Rest for an hour in a strainer. **4.** Place the fillets in a shallow dish, skin uppermost, and cover with vinegar. Refrigerate overnight.

The following day: 1. Take the fillets out of the vinegar. With your fingers, take off the thin skin that covers the skin: start by detaching it from the edge of the fillet with your nails, as if you were opening a sealed yogurt pot and pull gently (it comes off easily thanks to the vinegar) and discard. **2.** Place a makisu on a cutting board. **3.** Spread the plastic wrap onto it and tuck the edges under the makisu so that it stays put. **4.** Place a whole fillet in the middle of the wrap. If the fillet is thick, cut diagonally into 3 to 5 pieces, holding your knife at an angle of 45° or less from the board and lay the slices in a line. **5.** After wetting your hands, shape a rough cylinder of rice about the length of the fillet and place it on the fish. Lift the edge of the makisu nearest to you with both thumbs, holding the wrap in place, and roll gently but firmly. **6.** Press the makisu firmly several times (see "How to make maki" on page 187). **7.** Open the makisu carefully without unwrapping the wrap. **8.** Discard the wrap. Cut the sushi with a wet knife. Serve with wasabi or freshly grated ginger and soy sauce.

Bejetarian sushi no moriawase

Assorted vegetarian sushi

Wet your hands and make rice balls (see "How to make
nigiri" page 186). Prepare the garnish of your choice,
shaping them so that they sit on top of the rice balls without
sliding off. **2.** To fry tofu, use Chinese tofu instead of
Japanese; it's firmer and easier to cook. Cut into thin slices
and fry with a drop of sesame oil or vegetable oil, in a
nonstick skillet. Grate the ginger and place a pinch on the
tofu. **3.** For the garnishes that "roll" or don't sit well on the
rice ball (green peas, olives, etc.), wrap each rice ball
horizontally with a strip of nori slightly higher than the rice
ball, so that it makes a higher edge. For thin, round, stick-like
garnishes (green beans), cut small strips of nori that you
wrap around the garnish and the rice, holding them together
like a belt.

Don't forget that sushi should be eaten in a single bite.
Make sure each rice ball and its garnish are the right size.
Experiment and enjoy!

SERVES 1

8–9 oz vinegared rice
($^{1}/_{2}$–$^{3}/_{4}$ cup raw rice)

few strips of nori

fine green beans

cooked carrot

grilled tofu with nori

grilled tofu with
fresly grated ginger

red radish

brown mushroom

bamboo shoot

cherry tomato

takuan
(sweet pickled radish)

fresh peas

cucumber

black and green
olives, pitted and
cut into thin slices

green asparagus spears

MAKES 2 ROLLS

10 oz vinegared rice
(3/4 cup raw rice)

3 large tiger shrimp

pinch of salt

1/4 small cucumber

soy sauce

wasabi

pickled ginger
(optional),
see page 50

makisu

plastic wrap

Ebi to kyuri no bo-zushi
Bo-zushi of shrimp and cucumber

Skewer each shrimp lengthwise on a long wooded toothpick or wooden skewer to avoid curling when cooked. Drop the shrimp in boiling salted water. Cook until they turn pink. **2.** Peel the shrimp and butterfly-cut each, from the belly toward the back, without cutting all the way through to the back. Spread it out flat: you should get a V-shaped flat open shrimp. **3.** Wash and dry the cucumber and cut diagonally into very thin slices. **4.** Place the plastic wrap on the makisu, tucking the edges well underneath it. **5.** Place on the wrap, from left to right: a shrimp, tail downwards; a slice of cucumber; another shrimp, tail upwards... alternate so that you have a row of shrimp and cucumber in "stripes." It will be prettier if you place them diagonally (leaning a little to one side). **6.** Wet your hands and place a rough cylinder of rice on the row of shrimp and cucumber. **7.** Press gently with your fingers so that the rice sticks to the shrimp and cucumber. **8.** Holding the wrap in place, roll in one single motion, pressing firmly (see "How to make maki" on page 187). **9.** Unroll the makisu. Do not unwrap the wrap. **10.** Cut the roll into 8 pieces without unwrapping, with a wet knife—very sharp otherwise you won't be able to cut the plastic wrap. Then discard the wrap from each piece. **11.** Serve with soy sauce, wasabi, and pickled ginger.

VOYAGE TO THE LAND OF SUSHI

tokyo
東京

- Tokyo never sleeps: it is a teeming megalopolis. Millions of people; armies of shining new cabs; huge underground avenues; defiant skyscrapers; giant television screens. Armies of mobile phones with cameras, connected to the Internet. Vending machines everywhere, selling everything from cold and hot drinks, instant noodles, magazines, underwear... and here and there, in the middle of this frenzy, a small sanctuary of the fox (*inari jinja*), a tiny red house perched on a pole, hidden in a minute park behind the French Embassy, squeezed between two 30-story buildings. A gardener in *jika-tabi* (traditional working cloth shoes) carefully trims a tree. Small temples. Small houses. Small eating places run by elderly Japanese couples and noodle stands, which, at sunset, spring up among the skyscrapers. Tokyo is a complex city, where high technology and tradition are on friendly terms.

- The economical, financial, industrial, political and social capital of Japan is only a gathering of country people. If everybody comes to Tokyo, very few people are born here. Even today, people born in Tokyo and whose father and grandfather were born in Tokyo are called *Edokko*. Everybody gets lost here—other than the main avenues, the streets have no names. To travel in this huge urban center can be a nightmare. When you take a cab, you say: "turn left after the florist" or "turn right before the fish store." This labyrinth is an inheritance from the past, when the Shogun ruled Edo. After having built the biggest palace in the world, the Tokugawa Shoguns are said to have made this city into a maze to confine and stop the enemy from finding the palace.

- Visitors are always struck by the frenzy. Huge crossings called *scramble kosa* (scrambled crossing), where people cross in all directions at once; high-powered neon lights show the way to a bar, a restaurant, several night clubs, lighting this city where night never falls. The four major railroad and subway stations of Tokyo are the busiest of the country: Shinjuku, Ikebukuro, Shibuya and Tokyo Station.

- Tokyo Station covers 215,280 sq yards, with 3,800 trains carrying 1.75 million passengers daily. Every day 365 *shinkansen* (bullet trains) depart, an average of 30 per hour. So, in this megalopolis where a cup of coffee costs 500 yen, competition is fierce, and some revolving sushiya have set up loud speakers which, from morning to night, repeat in a multilingual high shriek: "One hundred yen! One hundred yen! Only one hundred yen a plate! One hundred yen sushi! One hundred yen sushi!"

CHIRASHI OF TOKYO FOR ONE,

SERVED AT TSURUHACHI.

THE VINEGARED RICE IS HIDDEN

UNDER A LAYER OF FISH AND SEAFOOD.

ANAGO, TUNA, SEA BREAM, OCTOPUS,

SQUID, *AKAGAI, KOHADA,* SMALL

SCALLOPS, MIRUGAI, ETC.

SASAMAKI KENUKI-ZUSHI WAS

ESTABLISHED IN 1702.

THE RESTAURANT HAS THREE

TABLES, TWELVE SEATS.

tokyo
東京

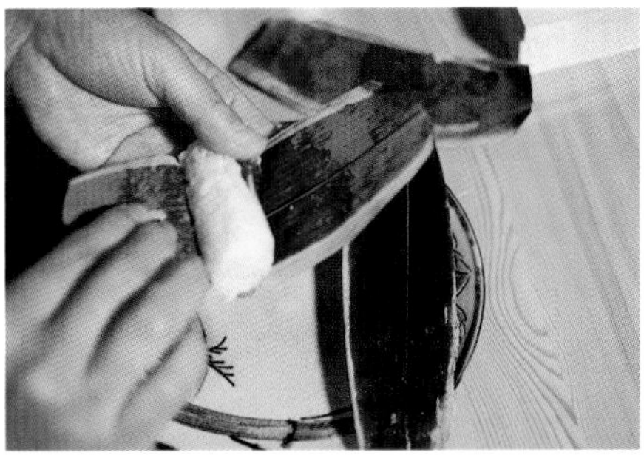

SASAMAKI-ZUSHI, OR SUSHI

WRAPPED IN BAMBOO LEAVES.

KOHADA, TAMAGO, SALTED *HIRAME*,

KANPYO ROLLS, DEPENDING ON

THE SEASON.

RIGHT

TAKE AWAY BOX OF *SASAMAKI-ZUSHI*

AND TRAY MENU SERVED IN THE

RESTAURANT: A PLATE OF SEVEN

SASAMAKI-ZUSHI, A BOWL OF

CLEAR SOUP AND TEA.

kyoto

京都

- *"Oo-ki-ni..."* These gentle and melodious syllables are how people in Kyoto say "thank you". Elsewhere in Japan, they just say *"arigato,"* but in Kyoto, everything is sweet, quiet and singing. All the images that come to your mind when you think of traditional Japan are from Kyoto: old temples with stone gardens, inviting meditation; alleys lined with black wooden houses, where women dressed in kimonos walk in dainty steps; narrow water ways, weeping willows, old fashioned stores where you sit on *tatami* to look at silks, fans, and lacquered combs, or even discreet bars, their names on a paper lantern, where you can savor little dishes that look more like exquisite paintings than food.

- Kyoto is the only place in Japan where the art of the *geisha* is taught. You may be lucky and see a *maiko* (literally "dancing child"), an apprentice *geisha*, walking to a *ryo-tei* (high-class restaurant where only known customers are accepted), to dance, sing and make conversation. When she finishes her apprenticeship, the *maiko* becomes a *geisha*—although they prefer to be called *geiko*, "child of the arts"—and changes her embroidered collar for a white one.

- *Kyo-ryori*, the beautiful cuisine of Kyoto, uses vegetables and plants from the mountains surrounding the city, playing on much more subtle and refined seasonings than those of Tokyo. It is said that the tea ceremony, *cha-no-yu* or *cha-do* ("space of tea" or "way of tea") in Japanese, was conceived by the Shogun to keep the samurai busy during peacetime. Small dainty sweets, a specialty of Kyoto, are eaten with the tea. Beautiful and delicious, they are still known all over Japan. One of my French friends found them so pretty she kept them to decorate her living room.

- Founded in 794, Heiankyo ("capital of peace and tranquility") was the cradle of the Imperial Court, and the capital of Japan until this function was transferred to Tokyo in 1868. This explains the cultural richness of Kyoto today. During the 16th century, the Shogun, Tokugawa Ieyasu, built the castle of Nijo, famous for its long "nightingale" corridors made entirely of wood, without a single nail, designed to signal the approach of spies and assassins. They make a faint noise, as delicate and charming as the voice of the nightingale, whenever somebody walks on them, even on tiptoe, rendering a furtive approach impossible. Kyoto is refined: as Edo loved *kabuki*, noisy and dramatic, Kyoto entertained itself with *no*, a form of theater of the Imperial Court where the actors move so slowly, the action is imperceptible.

- Kyoto was conceived like a chessboard ("Go Board" for the Japanese) making it easier to explore than Tokyo. The only city of Japan to have escaped the bombings during World War II, much of it remains intact. It is not surprising that Kyoto is the focus of envy: in Osaka, you will be told that the people of Kyoto are hypocrites; in Tokyo, that they are vicious. But Kyoto, the keeper of more cultural treasures than both cities combined, haughtily disdains such criticism.

A *MAIKO* (GEISHA APPRENTICE)

IN A STREET OF OLD KYOTO.

kyoto
京都

MAKING *SABA-ZUSHI*,

A SPECIALTY OF KYOTO, AT IZUU,

ESTABLISHED AROUND 1781.

THE MACKEREL IS CUT AND MARINATED

IN SALT AND VINEGAR. THE SUSHI IS

WRAPPED IN A LEAF OF KOMBU

SEAWEED AND IN A LEAF OF BAMBOO;

IT KEEPS FOR 24 HOURS AT ROOM

TEMPERATURE. TAKE-OUT OR SERVED

IN THE RESTAURANT.

A LADY OF KYOTO

MRS MIWAKO NOMA, OWNER

OF THE *RYO-TEI*, MOCHIZUKI.

MAKING *SASAMAKI-ZUSHI* OF
SEA BREAM AT HYOTEI. THE FISH
IS SLICED THINLY, THEN SALTED FOR
ONE HOUR. THE SUSHI IS WRAPPED
IN A BAMBOO LEAF—SAID TO HAVE
ANTISEPTIC QUALITIES—THE STALK
IS FOR DECORATION BUT ALSO HELPS
TO MAINTAIN THE SHAPE.

ROKUON-JI KINKAKU-JI IN WINTER.

THANKS TO THE NOVEL BY YUKIO

MISHIMA, THE GOLDEN TEMPLE OR

GOLDEN PAVILION IS ONE OF THE

BEST-KNOWN MONUMENTS OF JAPAN.

kyoto
京都

NISHIRI, A 150-YEAR-OLD STORE

FAMOUS FOR ITS PICKLES.

kyoto
京都

KYOTO IS KNOWN FOR ITS PICKLED

VEGETABLES (*TSUKEMONO*)

ABOVE SUSHI OF *TSUKEMONO*

(SUSHI ROLLED IN TURNIP TIED WITH

MIBUNA, EGGPLANT AND CUCUMBER,

CHINESE CABBAGE, TURNIP, TURNIP

LEAF AND CARROT, PICKLED

EGGPLANT, MOUNTAIN FLOWERS,

RED RADISH, FERMENTED TURNIP.

CENTER PICKLED TURNIP.

BELOW FERMENTED TURNIP.

THE DOTONBURI AREA IN OSAKA.

LEFT **KANIDORAKU, A RESTAURANT**

FOR CRAB—CRAB SASHIMI, CRAB STEW,

FRIED CRAB, CRAB SOUP—BUT ALWAYS

SHELLED AND READY TO EAT!

osaka
大阪

HAKO-ZUSHI, A SPECIALTY OF OSAKA.

GRILLED ANAGO, SHRIMP, EGG,

SHIITAKE MUSHROOMS, MARINATED

SEA BREAM, MINCED GINGER.

EVERYTHING IS COOKED—AND EATEN

WITHOUT SOY SAUCE.

- *"Kyoto kidaore, Osaka kuidaore"* (in Kyoto you ruin yourself from dressing, in Osaka you ruin yourself from eating). Osaka is the second city of Japan, Tokyo's great rival. It was the first city to embrace the Industrial Revolution and lead Japan toward modernization. Sanyo, Sharp, Panasonic, are some of the companies famous today who started their worldwide expansion from Osaka.

- Osaka was founded in the 5th century, but the year 1585 was to mark its destiny. The Shogun Toyotomi Hideyoshi built what was then the biggest castle of the country, and the merchants followed the court. The sea and several major waterways allowed Osaka to become an important center for trade. Everything gathered here and everything left from it: mainly rice, but also sake, miso, shoyu, coal, oil, cotton, salt. Osaka fed the enormous mouth that was Edo. Boats carrying sake from Kyoto and Nara left the port of Osaka and sailed up the coast to the Bay of Edo. After unloading at Edo, they would continue north, and bring back seaweed from Hokkaido.

- Osaka's geographical situation gave it access to the riches of both the sea and the earth. Peopled by rich, hard-working, demanding and greedy merchants, its commercial position brought it the best produce of the entire country. This explains the variety of its cuisine and the impressive list of specialties, each more popular than the last. *Udon-suki*, a soup of thick wheat noodles and meat cooked at the table; *okonomi-yaki*, a fat pancake of vegetables, meat, fish, shrimp and anything you may want, also cooked at the table on a hot iron plate; *tako-yaki*, balls of a pancake mixture with a piece of octopus, sold at street stands; *battera*, a sushi of marinated mackerel, topped with a sweet sheet of *kombu* seaweed, pressed together ... these are just some of the specialities served in the thousands of small restaurants—all of them good—that jostle with each other in Osaka. Osaka has also given Japan some of its best chefs, such as Kiccho, whose writings are the bible of Japanese high cuisine.

- Despite its commercial calling, Osaka has a spiritual aura thanks to the Temple of Shitenno-ji, built in 592 by Prince Shotoku, who introduced Buddhism to Japan. Rebuilt several times, the temple today is only a concrete replica of the original. Nonetheless, neither Kyoto, with its thousands of temples, nor Nara, proud of its Buddhist heritage, possess such an exalted treasure. The temple is still considered the center of Japanese Buddhism, which doesn't stop it, on the 21st of each month, opening its doors to a bustling flea market.

二寸六分の懐石

吉野

鯗 すし

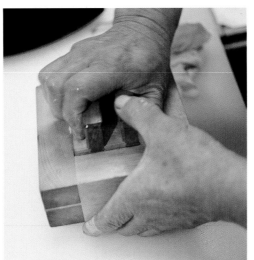

YOSHINO, OSAKA

MAKING OF *OSHI-ZUSHI* FOR ONE.

IT WILL KEEP FOR 24 HOURS AT

ROOM TEMPERATURE.

TAKOTAKE, OSAKA, ESTABLISHED 1831

THE *CHIRASHI* HERE IS VERY

ELABORATE. SEVERAL LAYERS OF

RICE AND FIFTEEN SUPPLEMENTARY

INGREDIENTS: *ANAGO*, SHRIMP,

SMALL MARINATED SEA BREAM,

SHIITAKE MUSHROOMS, *TAMAGO*, NORI,

SOBORO OF WHITE FISH AND SHRIMP,

BLACK MUSHROOMS, *SHISO, MITSUBA*...

nara
奈良

LEFT AN OLD MAN IN FRONT OF THE

DAIBUTSUDEN, THE GREAT TEMPLE

OF BUDDHA.

BELOW *KAKINOHA-ZUSHI* OR SUSHI IN

PERSIMMON LEAF, A SPECIALTY OF NARA.

THIS SUSHI, OF SALTED MACKEREL AND

SALMON, IS PRESSED AND WRAPPED

IN A PERSIMMON LEAF. THE BOXES OF

KAKINOHA-ZUSHI MAKE AN EXCELLENT

OBENTO (MEAL BOX).

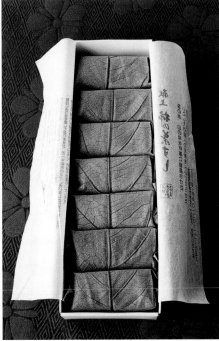

Founded under the name Heijyokyo "Citadel of Peace" during the 7th century, Nara was the capital of Japan from 710 to 784. At the time Japan was greatly influenced by all things Chinese—philosophy, religion, silk, soy sauce, miso and the first sushi. Nara has kept its status as a renowned cultural and Buddhist center.

A haven of calm and quiet, Nara hides invaluable treasures. Its park of 1630 acres shelters not only many famous temples, such as the religious complex of Todai-ji, where the Daibutsuden, the largest wooden edifice in the world, holds a 50-feet high bronze Buddha, but also a thousand deer, free denizens of the park. Here and there, wrinkled old ladies sell cookies for the deer in small makeshift stands. Nothing troubles the peace: a ripple perhaps, when an impatient deer tears away the tidbit from your hand.

A day with a sushiya | Kazuko Masui

Three years ago, I was sitting in a waiting room in Tokyo, leafing through a magazine when I suddenly started at the picture of a shrimp sushi. Red and white, straight and thin, it was an exquisitely elegant sushi. I found it so beautiful I went straight to Yokohama, a one-hour train ride from Tokyo, and discovered Jiro.

The lost sushi. For more than 60 years I have lived a love affair with sushi. I was seven years old when my mother and I went shopping. She had put on her nice kimono, and I had my going-out dress. We always went to the department store, and then we would have lunch in a restaurant. My mother didn't like the restaurant in the store. She would ask me: "Kazuko, what would you like?" "Sushi!" was invariably my answer. We always went to the same sushiya, at the end of a small alley. But that day, my mother cried out: "Oh Kazuko, it's closed!" I can still hear her little cry of disappointment … We never went back. War was to start some time after; the sushiya was burned down and my mother died at the end of the war.

Since I was 18, when I left home, until today, I have tasted sushi around the whole world. Tokyo, Osaka, Kyoto, Kobe, Fukuoka, Sapporo, Paris, London, Amsterdam, Rome, New York, Chicago, San Francisco, Honolulu, Pusan … I have been to more than 200 restaurants. But I had never found the sushi I was looking for: until that evening in Yokohama.

Master and disciple. The name of the restaurant is "Jiro, Yokohama-ten," because there is another Jiro, in the Sukiyabashi area in Tokyo. This one is the master, the oldest and most famous sushiya in Japan. At 78 years old, he is still in his restaurant every day. Jiro of Yokohama is his disciple.

His real name is Hachiro Mizutani and he is aged 56. He serves five seats at the counter and four at a little table next to it. He has no employees: his wife, Toshiko, does the service and cleaning. The restaurant opens at 5.00 pm and has two sittings every evening. It is barely 325 sq feet, including the kitchen. The *sushi-dane* are laid out in boxes of Japanese cypress, as beautiful as a painting.

The rice is white and it shines. Each grain is translucent. The knives, impeccable, are sharpened every day. "The knife is a part of my hand," says Mizutani the sushiya. Always face to face with his customers, with his knife, his *sushi-dane*, his wasabi, his shoyu and his rice, the sushiya performs a dance of the hands, practiced every day, a thousand times, before placing a single sushi on a small individual lacquered tray. Black lacquer, white rice, red, white, or grey fish, the scene is played by the contrast of colors, as striking as a sword, a very Japanese sense of beauty.

Through the looking-glass. I watch this play, made and delivered by the chef, only for me. The distance and time that separate the chef and his customer are practically non-existent. The fingers of the chef move toward me, the first three fingers of the hand, and place the sushi in front of me. My fingers move forward. The tuna is red; the rice is white. I can see the fat delicately spotting the meat. The chef's sauce is already spread on the fish: I do not dip the sushi in the shoyu. With only three fingers I bring this masterpiece into my mouth. Each grain of rice is distinct, the fish melts and the wasabi is a perfume. The vinegared rice and the fat of the fish are one, united in a same temperature. The sushiya is a magician.

With each sushi, I plunge deeper and deeper into the depths of the ocean. The tuna is the red meat of the sea. The silver shinko has a light taste and the texture of silk. The shrimp is a surprise; it is so sweet. The octopus leaves a smell of nuts. The eel melts in the mouth. The squid is soft. The sea urchin is rich, and its nori crunchy with taste.

Sitting at the counter, facing the chef, I sip on the tea served by the mistress of the house. Pleasantly hot, it washes away the fat of the fish. Jiro's sushi is for me, today, the best in the world. If my mother had tasted this beautiful sushi and delicious fish "Oh Kazuko, this is so good!" she would have said. And she would have smiled in total satisfaction.

A tour of the market. Hachiro Mizutani wakes up every day at 5.30 am. Winter and summer, he is awake just before the alarm clock rings. After getting dressed, he goes directly, without even drinking a glass of water, to Tsukiji, the fish market. It's far. He takes the train and the bus. After walking around the market, he breakfasts on fried, breaded pork cutlets or barbecue grilled beef. He leaves the market at 8.00 am and is back in Yokohama an hour later.

His "walk around the market" can't be done by anybody else because that is when he chooses the fish. There are thousands of suppliers in Tsukiji. He usually goes to five. He has his tuna specialist, his shellfish specialist, and his shrimp specialist, not to forget the vegetables. But if he finds something exceptional in a different shop, he buys. He doesn't bargain. Between professionals, it's a relationship based on trust.

He takes each fish in his hand. The traders don't like that. But that's the way it is. Jiro is also a professional. The atmosphere is tense. The freshness, the place of origin, the weight, the size and the price of the fish are important, of course. But it is only by touching that Jiro can know the fat, the meat, the smoothness and firmness of the animal.

Once back home, at 9:00 am, while he waits for the produce to be delivered from Tsukiji, he starts to prepare. He seasons the stock for the eel: sugar, mirin, water and a drop of shoyu to add color. Then he makes the chef's sauce. Equal amounts of shoyu and sake, and a drop of mirin, boiled and flambéed to burn the alcohol. seventy-five percent of the sushiya's work is in the preparation. At 9.30 am, the fish are delivered.

Perfect shrimp! Each morning, Jiro starts with the shrimp. Depending on the number of reservations, he prepares 15 or 20. Each shrimp weighs about one ounce. The wild shrimp are alive and jumping. If they weren't, the meat would be limp, and the 'miso', the liver of the shrimp, would smell bad and wouldn't be good to eat. High-quality shrimp, still hopping when at the sushiya's, take on beautiful colors of bright red and white when cooked, and its 'miso' is rich, sweet and melting. Jiro of Yokohama is one of the rare sushiya to use this liver; it is so difficult to use it well.

The shrimp are, like tuna, a quality *sushi-dane*, one that gives sparkle to the sushi platter. It is expensive, slightly less than tuna: the sushiya buys his shrimp at 400 yen and sells the sushi at 1000. Jiro has them throughout the year on the menu, but he changes the place of origin depending on the season: during the winter the shrimp come from the south, in Kyushu; May and June, from Hamanako; from July to October, the fishing areas gradually move up the archipelago, to Tokyo Bay. The shrimp of Hamanako and the Bay of Tokyo are at their best between the beginning of summer and fall.

To give the shrimp a nice straight shape, the sushiya skewers it on a bamboo stick, then cooks it in large amounts of strongly boiling water with a handful of salt. He cooks all the shrimp at once. Two minutes, not a second more. When the water becomes pink, the shrimp are taken out and thrown in ice water with ice to fix their color (which they lose when they cool naturally). Then he puts them, still in their shells, in the refrigerator at 41°F. He will take them out sometime before he commences the evening service so that they are back at room temperature, since as with all foods, shrimp sweeten and take on more flavor when they are warm. The sushiya peels them to order, just before making the sushi, taking care to leave the liver.

Small fish, will grow. The *shinko* is another important *sushi-dane*, even though it is a relative newcomer to the sushi scene. It is even more expensive than tuna; 70,000 to 140,000 yen per pound. *Shinko*, (literally "new child")—three make one sushi—needs a long preparation. But the sushiya has to have it: "Well, the *shinko*?" asks the connoisseur. "It's here!" answers the sushiya. Both welcome with the same enthusiasm this short and precious moment. Indeed, *shinko* fishing moves from south to north, and at each fishing point, the season lasts only about ten days. After that, it grows and becomes *kohada*. Thus, by moving up the archipelago, the fishing season is made to last a total of about a month throughout the archipelago.

Shinko has a delicate flavor and the texture of silk. It is firmed with salt, washed and marinated in vinegar. It is not salted directly, but soaked in salted water, because the salt damages its skin and meat. The "time of salt" and the "time of vinegar" are counted in seconds and must be scrupulously identical, because if one is longer than the other it will be stronger and will break the balance.

Kohada is used from the Edo era, and is the symbol fish of sushi. Its name changes with its size and age: after *shinko*, it becomes *kohada*, then *nakatsumi*, then *konoshiro*, as it grows. It is salted directly and marinated in vinegar. *Kohada* is a cheap and low-class fish, but the salt and vinegar change it into the star of *sushi-dane*.

The sushiya prepares the fish while they are still very fresh, starting with the ones that need to be cooked. He cooks the eel. He cooks the abalone in sake steam. He marinates the *kohada*. He opens the shellfish and prepares them. After lunch, he will open and slice the *hirame*, and finishes with the tuna, at 4.30 pm.

For lunch, Jiro has a bowl of Japanese or Chinese noodles nearby. It is the only time of the day when he sits. At 2:30 p.m., he is back at work, and makes the *tamago*, the sweet omelet. This takes about an hour. Six eggs, 14 oz of small shrimp, a piece of yam and sugar: he mashes all these ingredients in a type of mortar until the mixture is smooth, and then cooks it for about 40 minutes. It is said that the talent of a sushiya can be defined by the refinement of his *tamago*. Nowadays, many sushiya buy it ready-made. But Jiro makes his own. He puts the ginger, cut by a specialist in Tsukiji, into pickle.

Rice at body temperature. 3.30 pm. Jiro makes the rice for the first service. Depending on the number of reservations, he will cook between 6 and 7.5 go (1 go = 6 oz). In small quantities, otherwise the rice in the bottom of the cooker will be squashed. The rice must be well washed and immediately set to cook in water that is already hot; 15 minutes of cooking and 15 minutes of rest, to let the rice absorb the water.

Unlike rice that is eaten plain, sushi rice must not swell too much; otherwise it will not absorb the vinegar. The sushiya mixes in the seasoned vinegar very quickly and pours the rice in an *ohitsu* (a wooden receptacle which absorbs excess water), where it will cool for an hour, the time for the vinegar to penetrate into the heart of each grain. Jiro of Sukiyabashi, in Tokyo, the master of Hachiro Mizutani, "our" Jiro, says: "If the rice is not at body temperature, the sushi won't be good." His disciple goes even further: "Between a good fish and a bad rice, and a bad fish and a good rice, I'd choose the second. If the rice isn't good, you can't make good sushi."

Jiro lets his rice supplier choose the rice for him. The supplier knows what he wants. "The rice must shine with the vinegar. If the rice is weak, it won't become translucent when it absorbs the vinegar. Rice that will turn the color of smoked glass isn't good. Rice that sticks to the teeth isn't good either," says Mr Yanokura. Unyielding artisans and proud of their work, the two men are alike. They have known each other for 40 years, when they were both young apprentices. "Usually, the faster you eat the rice after harvest, the better it is," adds the rice merchant. "But sushi rice must mature for a year. That's why it has to be top quality, so that it doesn't lose taste. You need a solid rice, constant, which doesn't change with time. And, Jiro likes 'hard' rice. The one I give him is a mix of three Koshihikari rice, chosen from among 50, from the Nagano area. By mixing the three, you can maintain the quality through time. All rice is different. Good rice comes from a rice paddy filled with insects, worms and such nuisances: that's nature. I know the producers who make Jiro's rice. They are serious people, who produce little and don't skimp on their work. Their rice isn't ordinary, it's a difficult rice, practically unusable by an amateur. But when it's cooked by a real professional like Jiro, it's the best!"

Let the show start! 4.00 pm. Mrs Mizutani goes to the bank to deposit the income from the day before, picks up new notes for change, and comes to the restaurant. She cleans, rolls the damp hand towels, prepares the teapot and the cups. The tea is a mix of powder green tea and leaves, from the region of Shizuoka.

4.30 pm. Jiro works on the presentation of his *sushi-dane* in boxes of cypress wood (the most prized wood in Japan).

5.00 pm. He shaves and dresses. He puts on his white working clothes, his *tabi* (non-stretch socks, with a separation between the big toe and the other toes) and his *zori* (Japanese

traditional slippers). He hangs the *noren* outside the door and takes his place behind the counter. Jiro is ready. The restaurant can open. For four and a half hours, Jiro will stand, facing the customers, talking with them while he makes about 300 sushi. He never stops. He is alone on the scene, he cooks, serves, guides, intervenes, entertains, so that the evening should be as pleasant as possible, as much for the intellect as for the food. He knows he is constantly under observation; when he talks with the customers, he prepares the sushi and places them in front of them. But he watches them too. Without seeming to, he is sensitive to all their reactions. It's his job. The show will last for over four hours... the tension couldn't be maintained any longer. "As soon as I take the noren down, I become a different man," he says.

9.30 pm. closing time. It isn't always at the same time but it's usually the time to start cleaning. Jiro throws away all his cloths made of very thin white cotton, the smell of fish being too strong to be washed out. He washes the *sushi-dane* boxes, washes and scrubs the cutting board and the *ohitsu*. He takes back the damp towels to his home, where his wife washes, dries, rolls and steams them to sterilize them. Jiro doesn't use professional towel suppliers. He doesn't trust them. His towels are perfectly wrung out and rolled by his wife. The impeccably clean hot towel is a must for any self-respecting sushiya. This welcoming proof of hygiene is satisfying for the customer.

A life dedicated to sushi. 10.30 pm. At last, the couple close the shutters of the restaurant and walk back home. Jiro becomes Hachiro Mizutani, who drinks two glasses of whisky and water. He doesn't eat. He is asleep in a minute. That's why the next morning he takes a big breakfast.

Why is Jiro a master sushiya? The answer is easy: he knows his ingredients and all the regions of Japan. He knows that the way the fish has been caught is as important as the species, the place of origin and the season. A fish caught in a net will struggle, hurt itself and lose all its energy before dying. A fish killed immediately after being caught is best. But fish is not enough to make good sushi: all the ingredients—rice, salt, vinegar, the knives and the tea—and their temperature, the utensils, the least movement, are important. No detail can be neglected, and Jiro knows that perfectly well.

He is 5 ft 8 inches tall and weighs 128 lb. His weight hasn't chan-ged in 20 years. Born in 1947, the sixth of seven children, his father was a tangerine farmer. He began his apprenticeship when he was 15. For the first two years, he was only allowed menial tasks. The next four years, he didn't touch a single fish, nor even get close to a single grain of rice. But if this apprenticeship was long and hard, Hachiro Mizutani acknowledges how lucky he was to have learned the trade with two sushiya who have marked the recent history of sushi—Suekichi Yoshino and Jiro Ono. At the age of 30, he married Toshiko; the two families arranged the marriage. He became his own man with his own shop at the age of 46. Which means, when you think about it, that he has lived 42 years for sushi.

What to drink with sushi

SAKE

- Made with fermented rice, sake is a natural mate to sushi. Sake production is as complex as the production of wine. The cooked rice is fermented with its own yeast (*koji*), pressed, and filtered. Water is added to lower its alcohol content from 18 to 15 percent. It is pasteurized twice before bottling. A long-practiced tradition, alcohol is added only to sake sold in Japan. Polished rice is used. One determining factor of the quality of sake is its polishing ratio: the more it is polished, the more the sake is pure, refined and fragrant. The ratio mentioned on the label concerns the ratio of rice that is left after polishing: a ratio of 70 percent means that 30 percent of the rice was discarded by polishing. Therefore the lower the ratio, the higher the quality.

- There are two classes of sake: *futsu-shu* (ordinary) and *tokutei-meisho-shu* (superior). Within the latter are:

  1. *honjozo*: polishing ratio below 70 percent; alcohol added before pressing

  2. *junmai*: polishing ratio below 70 percent; made exclusively with rice, *koji,* and water

  3. *ginjyo*: polishing ratio below 60 percent; alcohol added before pressing

  4. *junmai ginjyo*: polishing ratio below 60 percent; made exclusively with rice, *koji,* and water

  5. *dai ginjyo*: polishing ratio below 50 percent; alcohol added before pressing

  6. *junmai dai ginjyo*: polishing ratio below 50 percent; made exclusively with rice, *koji,* and water

A *TOKKURI* OF SAKE AND AN *OCHOKO*.

A *TOKKURI* GENERALLY CONTAINS

ABOUT 1½ CUPS OF SAKE; AN *OCHOKO*,

1½–2½ TABLESPOONS.

- As with tea, sake served with sushi must not be too fragrant. Avoid the fruity aromas of a *dai ginjyo*, too close to apple and melon. The types of sake that match well with sushi are *junmai* and *junmai ginjyo*.

- Japanese restaurants usually have one sake, which is served cold (*hiya*, 41–60°F); at room temperature (*jo-on* or *shitsu-on*, 60–68°F); warm (*nuru-kan*, 86–104°F); or hot (*kan-zake* or *atsu-kan*, 113–122°F). Sake reveals different flavors and fragrances according to its temperature. A basic rule of thumb: the better the sake, the less it needs to be heated. A bad sake is practically undrinkable unheated. A *ginjyo* should be drunk cold or very slightly heated; it may be served with an ice cube. A dry sake is served cool; a sweet sake, heated. Sake is always heated in its *tokkuri* (the ceramic bottle in which it is served) immersed in boiling water. It is drunk from a *sakazuki* or *ochoko*, a small cup of 1½–2 tablespoons (or more), in lacquered wood for special occasions.

WINE

- Dry champagne, white Burgundy, white wine of the Loire or Alsace will go with most sushis. Only red tuna, somewhat close to red meat, can stand up to red wine. Wine does not go well with marinated shiny fish (*kohada*, sardine, mackerel), because it brings out an unpleasant metallic taste in the fish. But these fish can be very well matched with wine when they are raw.

- No single wine offers a perfect match to all sushi; which is why we have given you our favorites—a very personal choice—for each fish. You obviously can't change wines with each sushi, but feel free to experiment.

- Beware! Water brings out the fishy smell of fish and is ill advised with sushi.

KONACHA IS THE "POWDERED"

GREEN TEA OF THE SUSHIYA.

IT IS NOT REALLY POWDERED TEA,

BUT "CRUMBS." THIS "INSTANT" TEA

CAN BE POURED IMMEDIATELY,

SAVING TIME.

GREEN TEA

- Japanese green tea has a less flowery aroma and more bitterness than Chinese green tea. It matches sushi to perfection. There are four main types: *gyokuro* ("pearl of dew"), *sen-cha* ("infused tea"), *hoji-cha* ("roasted tea") and *kongo-cha* ("mixed tea") of which *genmai-cha* ("whole rice tea") is the most common.

- Cultivated in the shadow of reed screens, so as to to avoid direct sunlight, *gyokuro* is the best Japanese green tea. It is sweet, only slightly bitter and very delicate. It should be infused for 3 minutes in water at 122°F maximum. Its flavors are refined and long lasting, and its price is high: these factors make it unsuitable for sushi. *Hoji-cha*, medium quality tea that is roasted, and *genmai-cha*, green tea with steam cooked and dried rice, are both easy and pleasant to drink, but their smoky flavor make them unsuitable for sushi. *Sen-cha*, mid- to high-quality green tea, is nicely balanced between flavor, taste and bitterness: it is by far the most common tea in Japan.

- In fact, tea for sushi must not be too delicate or too rough. This is why sushi tea is often a blend of *gyokuro* and *sen-cha*, from different areas: for example, a bitter and strongly flavored tea from Uji, in the Kyoto area, with a tea from Sayama, of a characteristic jade-green color, and a more neutral tea from Shizuoka, which acts as a go-between. These mixtures are made by professional tea blenders.

- The sushiya buys the tea blend that he likes. He is allowed to serve tea to the customer only after 3 years of apprenticeship.

- Sushi tea must be ready immediately, which is why powder tea, *kona-cha*, is usually used. *Kona-cha* is not tea reduced to powder, but the fannings gathered after the processing (through a filter) of *sen-cha*. It must be very hot in order to neutralize the fat of the fish and cleanse the palate for the next sushi. It is served in big thick cups, with an *itozoko*, a type of base that retains the heat inside the cup and allows it to be held in the palm of the hand. In Japan, green tea is always served free.

- Green tea is said to be healthy. It contains vitamins (especially from the B group), minerals and a small amount of caffeine. But it is best known for its antioxidant effects beneficial to prevention of cancer and heart disease, thanks to its many polyphenols.

Sushi foods

Not to scale. The names are the most commonly occurring names in English.

Katsuo / Bonito

Sake / King Salmon

Tai / Red Sea bream

Hirame / Bastard Halibut

Shima-aji / White Trevally

Suzuki / Japanese Sea Bass

Karei / Marbled Flounder

Sumi-ika / Common Squid

Torigai / Cockle

Tako / Octopus

Nishin / Herring

Kisu / Japanese Sillago

Aji / Japanese Jack Mackerel

Saba / Pacific Mackerel

Sayori / Japanese Halfbeak

Kohada / Spotted Sardine

Anago / Sea Eel

Botan-ebi / Peony Shrimp

Ebi / Shrimp

Shiba-ebi / Shiba Shrimp

Shako / Mantis Shrimp

Maguro / **Northern Bluefin Tuna**

Hamaguri / **Hard Clam**

Awabi / **Abalone**

Mirugai / **Keen's Gaper**

Hotategai / **Scallop**

Kobashira / **Round Clam**

Hokkigai / **Surf Clam**

Tarabagani / **King Crab**

Zuwaigani / **Snow Crab**

Kegani / **Horsehair Crab**

Akagai / **Ark Shell**

Uni / **Sea Urchin**

Tsubugai / **Whelk**

Tara / **Cod**

Yugao / **edible podded snow peas**

Hirazayaingen / **edible podded snow peas**

Daikon / **Daikon radish**

Kanpyo

Shiitake / **Shiitake mushrooms**

Tamago / **Egg**

Kyori / **Cucumber**

What you should know...

HOW TO CHOOSE THE FISH

- In supermarkets, fish is often badly handled and damaged—but it's as easily bruised as an apple! Better to go to a specialist fish store.
- Sea bream, mackerel, horse mackerel, scad (*aji*): never buy these fish as fillets. It's too difficult to judge their freshness.
- Pick your fish whole and have the fishman scale and fillet it. The eye of the fish shouldn't be red, gray, or cloudy, but clear; the skin should be shiny. The fish should not bend or sag when the fishman picks it up.
- The meat of fresh tuna should be very red, not black, or bronze. Discard the gray matter on each side of the backbone, as well as the skin.
- Thaw frozen shrimp thoroughly before cooking. Do not buy precooked shrimp; they are usually too salty to be used for sushi (except for small shrimp with mayonnaise)

ESSENTIAL TOOLS

- A very sharp straight knife. Never use a serrated knife! Fish and sushi are easier to cut with a large knife: the blade should be at least 6–8-inches long.
- A *makisu*: a bamboo sushi mat to roll maki. You will find them in Japanese groceries, some Chinese stores and Western kitchen shops, and by mail order.

RICE STICKS!

- Wet everything that comes into direct contact with rice: spatula, knife, and bowls. Wipe your knife with a wet, well wrung-out cloth after each cut. The blade of the knife should always be clean, otherwise your next cut will be messy with bits of rice and fish that will transfer from the blade to whatever you are cutting.

orosu

How to cut fish

This cutting method works for salmon, mackerel, sea bream and horse mackerel, or scad (*aji*).
It does not apply to thin or long fish. If you ask your fishman to fillet the fish,
you can go directly to step 5.

Cut diagonally, from the back to the belly, top to bottom, behind the pectoral fin.

2. Repeat on the other side. Turn the knife and press, to break the backbone, and cut off the head and tail.

3. Cut the back of the fish above the dorsal fin, holding the knife flat, parallel to the board. Repeat this sideways movement, right above the bones. Repeat several times until you reach the backbone.

8. If you want to cut the fillet into thin slices, press firmly with one hand flat on the flesh, while you slice with the knife held at a 45° angle to the cutting board in the other hand.

4. Same procedure for the belly. In the part of the belly that is already cleaned, follow as much as possible the upper side of the ribs. Separate the fillet by cutting along the backbone. Turn the fish over and repeat steps 3, 4 and 5 on the other side. Discard the backbone.

卸す

7. Hold the skin at the tip of the fillet firmly between thumb and forefinger. Insert the knife and slide it along the skin to detach the flesh, pulling the skin toward you.

6. Cut each fillet in two, lengthwise, along the trace of the backbone.

5. Place the two fillets on the board. Cut off the parts on the belly which are black or too thin to be used. Run your fingers along the surface of the fillet to detect invisible pin bones and remove them with tweezers.

**MAKES JUST OVER
2 LB OF SUMESHI**

1 lb rice

2¹/₂ cups water

7 tbsp rice vinegar

1—4 tbsp sugar

1 tbsp salt

sushisu (sushi vinegar)
(can be found ready
to use in powder or
liquid form in certain
Asian grocery stores)

Sumeshi
Vinegared rice

Cooking rice is easy with an electric rice-cooker.
If you do not have one, use a nonstick heavy-bottom pan
with a well-fitting lid. It's better to use a gas hob, electric
hobs don't respond as quickly to changes of temperature.
However, if you only have electric, follow the instructions
in *italics*.

1. Wash the rice, and cover in a pan with water, bring to a
boil on maximum heat. As soon as the water is boiling and
the lid is rattling, turn the heat down to medium for 5 to 10
minutes; then reduce further to very low. *With an electric
hob, reduce the heat to very low, take the pan off the hob
and wait a little for the heat to lower before putting it back
on.* **2.** Let the rice simmer for 13 to 15 minutes on very low
heat, then turn the heat to high for 10 seconds (*longer for
electric*) so that there is a lot of steam before removing the
pan from the heat. **3.** Remove from the heat. Wait 10 minutes
before taking the lid off, so that the rice absorbs the steam
completely and becomes swollen and soft. **4.** If, when you
raise the lid, there is still some water on the surface, put the
lid back on quickly and wait another 10 minutes to let the
rice absorb all the steam.

How to prepare sumeshi

Use a Japanese rice (*koshihikari* or *sasanishiki*); it's expensive when imported from Japan, but cheaper when grown in California, Spain, Italy, or Korea. Always season the rice while hot. To "cut the rice" in Japanese means "to air", season and let it cool.

Sushi rice must be round-grain.

2. Put the rice in the saucepan and add twice its volume of water. Stir with one hand and drain the water. Repeat until the water is clear.

3. Add the cooking water (about 1⅓ to 1½ cups to 1 cup of rice). Follow the instructions for cooking rice on the facing page. A good lid is a must: steaming the rice at the end of cooking is an essential step.

8. The *sumeshi* is ready when no more steam rises from it, and it is warm to the touch but not hot.

酢飯

4. Your rice is well cooked if it is slightly unstuck from the sides of the pan and has a smooth surface with small holes.

7. The goal is to air the rice as quickly as possible while spreading the vinegar seasoning evenly. This quickens the evaporation of the water, and cools the rice: the rice takes on the luster characteristic of sushi rice.

6. "Cut the rice" by running the edge of a round wooden spatula across the rice, in a cross-hatching motion, and fold it without breaking the grains, while you pour small amounts of the vinegar mixture into it. If possible, have someone help you fan the rice to air it: in Japanese families, mother "cuts" the rice, while a child fans it with a fan or a newspaper!

5. Dissolve the sugar and salt in the vinegar. Transfer the hot rice into an *ohitsu* or a wet big bowl.

nigiru

How to make nigiri

Don't be disappointed if your nigiri are unshapely little balls and don't look anything like the ones at the sushiya. In Japan, nobody even tries to make nigiri at home. As for me, I make balls of rice, disregarding shape let alone perfection, put a slice of fish on top and vaguely press everything in both hands. The result is not pretty, but edible...

Prepare the wasabi in a small dish. Prepare a bowl of water with a little vinegar. Wet your hands. Take a slice of fish in the palm of one hand. Take some rice in the other hand.

2. Gently close your hand without squashing the rice, while shaking your hand to settle the rice.

3. Shape the rice into a ball in the palm of one hand, quickly to avoid sticking. The slice of fish is still in the palm of your other hand.

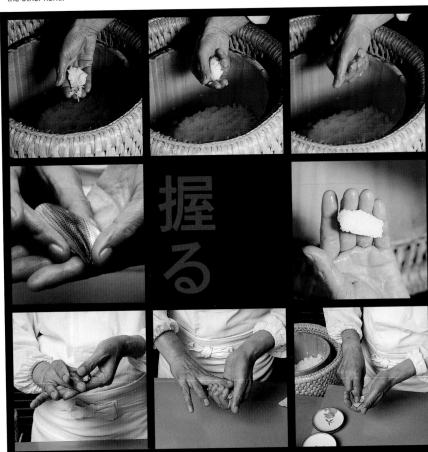

8. Turn the sushi, press again. Line up neatly on a plate, wipe off the bits of rice sticking everywhere! Serve with pickled ginger and soy sauce.

4. You should have an oval cylindrical rice ball, but at this stage it doesn't have to be perfect (like this one!).

7. Press the sushi on all sides, using the first two fingers or the thumb and forefinger of one hand. The palm of the hand holding the sushi still serves as a base for it to sit on. Repeat until the nigiri is well shaped and the rice holds together.

6. While half closing your hand, press on the rice ball with the first two fingers of your now free hand.

5. While holding the rice ball in the hollow of your hand, apply some wasabi (optional), with the tip of the forefinger of the same hand, on the slice of fish still held in your other hand, as though applying face cream. Then place the rice ball on the fish slice.

How to make maki

It's best to use a *makisu* but if you don't have one, fold a big sheet of aluminium foil in four, so that you have a stiff square you can roll with. This will be more difficult to handle than a *makisu* and your maki will be a little soft, but it is a possible alternative.

Cut the fillings into thin sticks or slices. Place a makisu horizontally in front of you. Place a sheet of nori on it, rough side up. Wet your hands and form a cylinder with the rice without squashing the grains.

2. Spread the rice on the nori, in a thin layer. Leave a border of nori at the top and bottom.

3. Dig a shallow groove horizontally down the middle of the rice. Dab on some wasabi. Place the filling in it. If the sticks are shorter than the nori, align them in a single line, overlapping a little.

8. Cut the rolls the same size. Usually, you press them lightly together to form a nice rectangle. Serve with pickled ginger and *shoyu*.

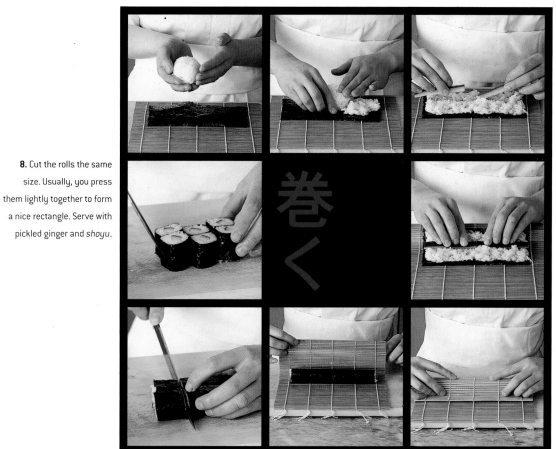

4. Lift the edge of the *makisu* that is nearest you with both thumbs and start rolling firmly, holding the filling in place with the tips of the other fingers.

7. Holding the roll firmly with your fingers, cut in a single motion without sawing (if your knife is sharp and wet, this should be easy).

6. Unroll the *makisu*. Place the maki on the cutting board. Wet a sharp knife with some water and vinegar.

5. When you have an almost complete roll, press several times over the length of the *makisu*. Roll completely and press, more firmly this time. Do not be afraid to let the rice and filling stick out from the sides—just tuck them in.

How and where to eat sushi
the best and worst of the sushi restaurant

WHAT TO DO IN A SUSHI RESTAURANT

1. As soon as you lift the *noren* (short "curtain" hanging above the door, a sign that the restaurant is open) and walk in, the sushiya welcomes you with a loud cry of "*Irasshai-mase*" (welcome).

2. You are given damp towels, hot in winter, cool in summer. The waiter asks what you would like to drink. Normally you order the food directly from the sushiya, as you go. The "menu," a list of available *sushi-dane*, is hung on the wall behind the sushiya, although outside Japan, there is often a menu for Westerners.

3. The chopsticks of plain white wood are placed on the counter in front of you, horizontally, on a *hashioki* (chopstick stand), the tips pointing to the left.

4. There is also a small plate for the shoyu.

5. Except in very high-class sushiya, the fish are displayed in a refrigerated glass cabinet, in whole fillets.

6. Ask the sushiya what is good today.

7. The sushiya places in front of you a small board of plain, varnished or lacquered wood and some pickled ginger. He may also serve you directly on the plain wooden counter.

8. Do not overfill your shoyu dish. Just pour a small puddle.

9. Take a nigiri in your fingers or with the chopsticks. Turn it upside down and dip the tip of the fish gently into the shoyu.

10. Do not bite into a sushi. Except for some maki, sushi is bite-size.

11. If you wish, you can ask for one nigiri ("*ikkan*"), or two ("*nikan*"). Or ask for less rice ("*shari sukuname*") or no wasabi ("*sabi nuki*").

12. Sometimes the wasabi is too strong. This happens in the best sushiya. It is perfectly acceptable to shed a few tears.

13. In Japan, green tea, ginger, wasabi, and shoyu are free and unlimited.

14. Eat what you want as much as you like. Don't be shy—ask if you don't know. Rare items are often hidden away, but regulars know Oyakata has them. Observe the other customers.

15. Ask for the bill—"*oaiso*" (the amiability) or "*okanjo*" (the account). If you wish to make a linguistic effort, add "*gochiso-sama*" (it was a feast).

17 WAYS TO SPOT A BAD SUSHIYA:

1. If the refrigerated glass cabinet and the cutting board are carelessly cleaned—wet, with bits of rice, nori and water, leave immediately! Sushi is raw fish. If only for your health, everything should be spotless.

2. There is a fishy smell in the restaurant. This means their fish is not fresh or that the restaurant is not clean.

3. The damp towel leaves you with wet hands.

4. The pickled ginger is very red or pink (artificially colored) and very sweet.

5. The rice is long grain.

6. The fish are piled haphazardly or pre-cut into slices.

7. There are raw freshwater fish or herring (danger of parasites).

8. The tuna is purple, black, green or very dark red (not fresh) or light red (different species).

9. The toro is so fatty it is white.

10. The white fish are yellow, gray, and/or dry around the edges.

11. When slicing shiny fish, especially mackerel, the part of the meat not exposed to the air is dry, yellow or gray (it is perfectly normal when the surface of the meat is yellow or gray because of being soaked in vinegar).

12. Scad or horse mackerel (aji) is served with wasabi (except when specifically requested).

13. The shellfish, usually displayed un-shelled in the glass case, are always thrown hard, just before being served, against the cutting board to make sure they are still alive. If they don't react or "shrink" when hitting the board they are flabby and very dead (and dangerous!).

14. The squid and octopus are dry around the edges and yellowish.

15. The nigiri or maki crumble as soon as you touch them.

16. The nigiri, served in pairs, are not of the same size.

17. The miso soup contains little miso.

TRUE OR FALSE?

What seems to be common practice outside Japan, but shouldn't be:

1. The restaurant also serves cooked food (yakitori, tempura, sukiyaki). This is against all rules of sushi, since the smells of cooked fat pollute sushi. The only hot dish served in a real sushiya is soup.

2. There is no counter, only tables.

3. The chopsticks are lacquered or plastic.

4. The sushiya advises salmon, a mediocre fish, since most of it is farmed (it is very good if wild).

5. Soup is served at the beginning of the meal, with a spoon and no lid, when it should be drunk directly from the bowl and at the end of the meal.

6. The sushi platter only contains tuna, salmon, shrimp and a few maki. Westerners are used to these sushi, which are also economical since they keep better than most.

THE GOOD SUSHIYA

1. If he suggests chu-toro, aji or mackerel, he is probably taking you seriously and suggesting the best he has, since most sushiya outside Japan don't suggest these fish to Westerners.

2. The tuna is a beautiful red, not too dark or too light; the white fish are of a good translucent white, opaque or pink color, depending on the fish; the squid is milk white. The unshelled shellfish, when thrown hard against the cutting board, react immediately and contract strongly (like when you drop some fresh lemon juice on raw oyster). The faster they "shrink" the fresher and crunchier they are. All the ingredients shine with natural moisture and freshness.

3. The price—unfortunately, high-quality fresh fish, good rice, and a renowned sushiya are not cheap. Even if some restaurants go overboard, you can't reasonably except to eat good sushi without paying the price.

Glossary

You may have noticed that Japanese is not an easy language. To make it easier to read for non-Japanese, it is often transcribed into the Roman alphabet. Unfortunately, the transcription does not follow strict rules. This is especially confusing with long vowels, as in "big mountain" pronounced "ooyama," but which may be written, ooyama, ohyama, ōyama, or oyama. In this book, we have omitted all indication of long vowels, except in the glossary and the acknowledgments, as it can change the meaning of a word: "anko" is a sweet soybean paste, whereas "ankō" is monkfish!

Agari Tea.

Aka-mi Literally "red flesh" and usually tuna.

Arigatō Thank you.

Bō-zushi Cylindrical sushi, shaped like a thick stick—literally, "stick sushi."

Chirashi or **chirashi-zushi** Literally, "scattered sushi."

Daikon Giant white or long radish, also called daikon radish.

Dashi Stock, made with dried shaved bonito, kombu seaweed or dried shiitake mushrooms.

Edo-mae-zushi Sushi of Edo—literally, "sushi in front of Edo."

Futomaki Thick roll containing generally five sweet and salty fillings—literally, "thick roll."

Gari Pickled ginger in sushi language.

Gohan Plain cooked rice.

Gunkan-maki Literally "warship roll"—it takes its name from its shape.

Hako-zushi Sushi pressed in a square box and cut—literally "box sushi."

Hashi Chopsticks. Chopsticks at the sushiya are not reusable. They are in plain white wood of different quality.

Hashi-oki Chopstick rest, made of wood or ceramic.

Hikari-mono Shiny fish –literally "thing that shines."

Hiya Unheated sake.

Hōchō Kitchen knife.

Hoso-maki Long thin roll usually with one filling, cut into six pieces—literally "thin roll."

Ita-mae Japanese cook—literally "in front of the board." Often wrongly used to designate the sushiya. "*Ita-mae-san*" when you are talking to the person.

Kabuki Type of Japanese opera in which the actors are all male. Popular entertainment developed during the Edo era (1603–1867).

Kanpyō Dried green gourd, cooked, sweet and salty. Always served in *hoso-maki*. Also a must in *futomaki*.

Kan or **atsu-kan** Heated sake.

Kōji Fermented rice used to make shoyu and sake.

Kome Uncooked rice.

Kudasai Vaguely translates as "please." Actually means "give to me," without being uncouth. A convenient word, as it only needs to be placed after whatever you want, e.g. toro *kudasai*, mackerel *kudasai*, etc.

Kyūri Cucumber. Japanese cucumber is smaller and more aromatic than European or American varieties.

Maki-mono or **maki-zushi** Sushi rolled in nori.

Makisu Small bamboo mat used exclusively to roll sushi.

Mana-ita Cutting board.

Me-negi Literally "onion sprout," type of very thin scallion.

Mibuna Green plant from the region around Kyoto and Osaka.

Mirin Sweet filtered liquid, made with rice alcohol and used to sweeten and flavor some dishes.

Miso Salty fermented soybean paste, generally used to make miso soup.

Mitsuba Aromatic herb.

Moromi Mixture of steamed soybeans, roasted crushed wheat, fermented rice, water, and salt, which, once fermented becomes soy sauce.

Neta Mistakenly but commonly used term to designate the supplementary ingredient or filling of sushi, cut or not. The correct word is *tane* (see below).

Nigiri-zushi Slice of fish lightly pressed on an oblong ball of vinegared rice.

Nikiri Sauce made of shoyu and sake, of which the sushiya flambées the sake. Sometimes served by sushiya instead of shoyu.

Nishin Herring.

Noren Short ungathered curtain, in thick cotton or linen, displaying the logo or name of the establishment. Hung above the entrance when the place is open, put away inside when closed.

Nori Dried, often roasted, sheet of seaweed.

Oaisō The bill or the check.

Obentō Take-away box. The *obento* was a take-away meal for travelers in days when most journeys were on foot. Balls of rice would be wrapped in thin bamboo bark. Today, boxes come complete with chopsticks, toothpick, hand wipe, and of course, hot and cold food, especially sushi.

Oboro Sweet and salty dry flaky paste made with white fish, shrimp, round clams.

Ochoko Small cup for sake, generally contains about $1\frac{1}{2}$–$2\frac{1}{2}$ tablespoons.

Okozara Small plate, especially designed for soy sauce to dip sushi.

Onegai-shimasu "Please"—literally, "I hope from you." More formal and versatile than *kudasai*.

Osai-bashi Kitchen chopsticks.

Oshi-zushi Literally "pressed sushi."

Osushiya-san Polite form of address to the sushiya.

Oyakata Chef sushiya, generally the oldest man behind the counter. The same word is used to address the person directly (do not add *san*).

Sabi Wasabi in sushi language. *Sabi-nuki* means "without wasabi."

Sakazuki Small sake cup. Can also be a bigger shallow cup made from lacquered wood, in which sake is passed around for a celebration.

Sanma *(Cololabis saira)* Pacific Saury—common Japanese fare, broiled. Popular in fall when it is most appreciated.

Sansho *(Zanthoxylum piperitum)* Highly aromatic non-pungent spice, also called Szechuan pepper.

Sara (or politely, *o-sara*) Plate.

Sashimi Raw fish or seafood (or sometimes beef, chicken), sliced, without rice; served with wasabi or freshly grated ginger and soy sauce.

Saya-ingen Green beans; *hira-zayaingen* are edible podded snow peas, also known as sugar peas, Chinese peas, and mangetout. Not the same however as snap beans.

Shari Rice in sushi language.

Shiitake Mushrooms, sometimes called Chinese mushrooms, used fresh, or dried and soaked in water.

Shinko Small *kohada* or spotted sardine. Named *shinko* from birth to a body length of 2 inches; *kohada* when $4\frac{3}{4}$–5 inches long; and *nakatsumi* and *konoshiro* from $6\frac{1}{4}$ inches and longer.

Shinko Pickled daikon radish (see Daikon above).

Shiro-mi White fish—literally "white flesh."

Shiso *(Perilla frutescens)* Aromatic herb, sometimes called Chinese basil, known in Asia as a remedy against allergies. Often used with seafood (crab, shellfish) known to be allergenic, and raw fish.

Shōyu Soy sauce.

Shun Best season to eat, as opposed to the best fishing season. The best fishing season is the season during which there is the most fish to be caught, whereas *shun* is often the opposite, when the fish is rare. The *shun* of *shinko* only lasts for 10 days in a given place. The *shun* of a fish is often defined by the spawning season: the eggs take away the strength of the fish, making it dry and tasteless.

Soboro (see *oboro*).

Su Vinegar.

Suehiro-maki or **temaki** Hand-rolled cone-shaped roll—without using a *makisu* (see above).

Sumeshi or **sushimeshi** Vinegared rice for sushi.

Sushi-su Sushi vinegar.

Sushiya Sushi cook, also sushi restaurant.

Tamago Literally, "egg." It designates the sweet and salty "omelet," *tamago-yaki*, in sushi language.

Tane or **sushi-dane** Sushi supplementary ingredient or filling.

Tara Pacific cod.

Te-maki see *suehiro-maki* above.

Tōfu Unfermented soybean curd, usually shaped into a rectangular cube, sometimes called soy cheese. Japanese tofu is whiter and softer then Chinese, which has a firm solid texture. Japanese tofu is eaten raw or cooked. Chinese tofu is usually cooked.

Tokkuri Ceramic container in which to heat and serve sake.

Tsukemono Salted and pickled vegetables, more or less fermented. Mainly eaten with rice.

Tsume Salty sweet sauce, made from very reduced cooking stock of certain foods. The sushiya spreads it on cooked **sushi-dane** such as octopus, shako, eel and shellfish with a wide brush.

Ukiyoe Literally, "image of a floating world." Multicolored engravings on wood. Popular posters of the times, *ukiyoe* represented scenes of life in Edo. After 1868, *ukiyoe* were much in demand in Europe, especially in France, and influenced artists of the post-Impressionist period (Toulouse-Lautrec, Degas, Van Gogh).

Wasabi Sometimes called Japanese horseradish; grated root used with sashimi and sushi.

Yugao Green gourd—literally, "face of the evening."

Index

Acknowledgments

Our thanks go first to all those in France without whom this book would have never seen the light of day, starting with Frédérique Sarfati, who believed in the project from the very first, Dominique Dumand who directed it, Isabelle de Jaham who was an angel of patience, Odile Zimmermann who covered up our blunders, Philippe Marchand and Emilie Greenberg who gave it color and life, and Laurence and Gilles Laurendon, the instigators of this project.

To the wonderful sushiya of Japan, who let us share their art and knowledge: Tsuruhashi (Tokyo); Jiro Yokohama-ten (Yokohama); Sushi-zen (Sapporo); Izu, Hyotei, Nishiri, Nontaro (Kyoto); Yoshino, Takotake (Osaka), as well the suppliers of fish—and their fish—who agreed to be photographed: Nishichu, Ishiyama, Oyo, Matsuhiro, Yamatoshi, Maruju (Tsukiji, Tokyo).

Our thanks also go to:
• Those who, by their work, supply our tables (and counters) everyday with their familiar but precious gifts: Yamamoto Nori-ten (nori); Sasaki Shoten (ginger); Kichie Shioya (wasabi); Kikkoman Corporation (shoyu); Murayama Zoshu KK , Mitsukan Group (vinegar); Sakai Hamono Kyokai (knives).
• Rokuonji and Seikadobunko for the use of their archives.
• Toyomitsu Nakayama, Maiko Kato, Taichi Ando, Masao Karasuyama, Jean-Pierre Lopez of the Poissonnerie du Dome, who put a lot of hard work into the recipes.
• Hachiro Mizutani, who let us share the life of a sushiya.
• Kazunori Kiyotsune, of the Japan Prestige Sake Association for the choice of sake.
• Isabelle and Robert Vifian of Tan Dinh for the choice of wines.
• And to the great experts Yukio Morooka, the previous Oyakata of Tsuruhashi, Doctor Ichiro Yamamoto, Professor Emeritus of the University of Kitazato, whose studies on algae and cancer were a revelation, Miwako Noma, architect and owner of the ryo-tei Mochizuki, who posed with all the grace that symbolized her city, Kyoto (see page 155), and Yohei Maruyama whose photos of sushi first gave us the idea for this book.
• Our friends and family, who never failed us in their love, friendship, and good humor, during the years it took to conceive and produce this book: Yoshiharu Tsuboi, Tei Shimizu, Ryuichi Iida, Keiko Obi, Setsuko Chikamori, Haruhiko and Iichiro Gushima, Shigeki, Kiyoko and Noriko Masui, Danielle and Andre Petit, and, last but not least, Laurent, Nona, Guillaume and Nicolas.

For those of you who wish to know more about sushi, sushiya and their fish, Edo or Japanese knives, and who can read Japanese:

神田鶴八　鮨ばなし　師岡幸夫 Kanda Tsuruhachi Sushi-banashi, by Yukio Morooka.

鮓・鮨・すし　すしの事典　吉野昇雄 Sushi, sushi, sushi Sushi no Jiten, by Masuo Yoshino.

すきやばし次郎　旬を握る　里見真三 Sukiyabashi Jiro, Shun wo Nigiru, by Shinzō Satomi.

江戸前ずしの悦楽　「次郎よこはま店」の十二ヵ月　早川光 Edomae-zushi no Seiraku "Jirō Yokohama-ten" no Jūnikagetsu, by Hikaru Hayakawa.

江戸の町　内藤昌　イラスト穂積和夫 Edo no Machi, by Masaru Naito, Illustrations by Kazuo Ineseki.

江戸名所図会　斎藤幸雄・斎藤幸孝・斎藤幸成 Edomeishozukai, by Yukio, Yukitaka and Yukinari Saito.

マグロの生産から消費まで　小野征一郎編著 Maguro no Seisan kara Shōhi made (Tuna: from the production to the consumer) written and edited by Seichiro Ono.

日本産魚類大図鑑　益田一・他・編 Nihon san Gyorui Daizukan (Illustrated Encyclopeadia of Japanese Fish), written and edited by Hajime Masuda.

堺打ち刃物を語る　諸岡博熊・竹内利江・共編 Sakai Uchi Hamono wo Kataru (An oral history of the knives of Sakai) edited by Hirokuma Morooka and Toshie Takeuchi.

Our compliments to the authors of www.fishbase.org, an amazingly complete database on fish around the world (it's a pity shellfish, crustaceans and cephalopods are missing!), and Peter Warshall and Dan Imhoff on www.wholefoods.com "A 3,000-Year History of Our Most Modern Oilseed".

Photographic credits